T0316680

SIR GAWAIN

AND THE

GREEN KNIGHT

Sir Gawain
and the
Green Knight

Translated into Modern English

by Thomas Wayne

Algora Publishing
New York

Library of Congress Cataloging-in-Publication Data —

Library of Congress Cataloging-in-Publication Data

Names: Wayne, Thomas, translator.
Title: Sir Gawain and the green knight / translated by Thomas Wayne.
Other titles: Sir Gawain and the Green Knight. English.
Description: New York, New York : Algora Publishing, [2020] | Translated
    from the Middle English. | Summary: "Before there was Game of Thrones,
    there was a sophisticated Arthurian romance replete with brave knights,
    noble ladies, temptation, seduction, blame, shame, and a memorable
    beheading game in an obscure Middle English dialect. This new edition is
    closely translated from the original, presenting the delightful and
    insightful story of a flawed hero, and a fascinating villain or two,
    with verve and vital energy"— Provided by publisher.
Identifiers: LCCN 2020000539 (print) | LCCN 2020000540 (ebook) | ISBN
    9781628944105 (trade paperback) | ISBN 9781628944112 (hardcover) | ISBN
    9781628944129 (pdf)
Subjects: LCSH: Gawain (Legendary character)—Romances. | Arthurian
    romances.
Classification: LCC PR2065.G3 A3878 2020 (print) | LCC PR2065.G3
(ebook)
    | DDC 821/.1—dc23
LC record available at https://lccn.loc.gov/2020000539
LC ebook record available at https://lccn.loc.gov/2020000540

PREFACE

Sir Gawain and the Green Knight is not without a myriad of modern translations. The 14th-century Arthurian romance commonly attributed to the anonymous "Pearl Poet" offers a tale of deception, honor, temptation, and failure, themes that continue to tantalize modern readers. The eponymous Gawain's struggle to adhere to his ethical values and his failure due to the will to live are concepts that are universal. It is not surprising that the Middle English poem remains a requisite for lovers of literature, and therefore many translations are readily available for readers to choose from.

However, many translators fall short on delivering an accessible Sir Gawain that remains true to the text. Some sacrifice formal equivalence to capture a semblance of the original's alliterative verse; others impose their own style and, in their attempts to modernize the text, bastardize the meaning; and some go the prosaic route, commendable for capturing its essence yet losing poetic form. While translation by nature will always require some extent of failure — perfection is never attainable when converting content from its original language to one it was not intended for — it is important for translators to leave behind little trace of their presence, to fail as little as possible.

1

The accuracy of this *Sir Gawain* comes out of an awareness of previous translations' shortcomings and a meticulous and arduous effort to veritably fill the gaps others have left.

Dr. Thomas Wayne has found the right balance between fidelity and metaphrase, staying faithful to the message without surrendering precision toward word meaning. Although the alliterative verse and "bob-and-wheel" structure have only been retained when correct word choice affords that opportunity, this process leaves readers with a poetic Sir Gawain in modern English that does not present erroneous substitution for the sake of style. The translation accentuates the medieval essence of the original text; decisions to use archaic cognates and keep the original's tense shifts and second person pronouns — "thee," "thou," "ye," etc. — help preserve the source material and allow readers to easily escape into the fantastical setting of Arthurian legend.

I had the opportunity to play a small role in assisting Dr. Wayne with this endeavor, which offered me firsthand insight into the process. If I were to sum up Wayne's approach to translation in one word, it would be assiduity. Where other translators take shortcuts to eschew the complexities of the Northwest Midland dialect, he confronts them with careful contemplation. I spent weeks with Wayne examining his second handwritten draft line by line, perusing dictionaries and various academic resources, and discussing definition, connotation, context, and word choice. What emerged from this diligent work is a precise translation of Sir Gawain that allows the original to breathe, and I am proud to have taken part in this journey.

Nathan Lewis, B.A.
Florida Gulf Coast University

FITT 1

I

1.   Since the siege and the assault was ceased at Troy,
       The burg breached and burnt to brands and ashes,
       The man who the plots of treason there wrought
       Was tried for his treachery, the truest on earth.
5.   It was Aeneas the noble and his high kind
       That then subdued provinces, and patrons became
       Well-nigh of all the wealth in the western isles.
       When rich Romulus to Rome reaches quickly,
       With great boasting that burg he builds up first,
10.   And names it with his own name, as it now has;
       Ticius to Tuscany and dwellings begins,
       Langobard in Lombardy lifts up homes,
       And far over the French flood Felix Brutus
       On many banks full broad Britain he settles
15.   with delight;
             Where war and wrack and wonder
             At times have dwelt therein,
             And oft both bliss and blunder
             Full swiftly have shifted since.

II

20.	And when this Britain was built by this knight rich,
	Bold men bred therein that loved strife,
	In many a turbulent time that wrought suffering.
	More marvels in this land have befallen here oft
	Than in any other I know of, since that same time.
25.	But of all that dwelt here, of Britain's kings,
	Ever was Arthur the gentlest, as I have heard tell.
	Therefore an event on earth I intend to show,
	One strange in sight some men might hold,
	And an outrageous adventure, of Arthur's wonders.
30.	If you will listen to this lay but a little while,
	I shall tell it at once, as I heard it in town,

with tongue,
As it is stood and placed
In story stout and strong,

35.	

With lawful letter locked,
On earth it has lasted long.

III

	The king lay at Camelot upon Christmas
	With many lovely lords, men of the best,
	Reckoned of the Round Table all those rich brethren,
40.	With rich revel a-right and reckless mirth.
	There tourneyed men by times full many,
	Jousted full jollily these gentle knights,
	Then came to the court carols to make.
	For there the feast was alike full fifteen days,
45.	With all the meat and the mirth that men could devise;
	Such shouting and glee glorious to hear,
	Dear din by day, dancing at night,
	All was the height of happiness in the halls and chambers
	With lords and ladies, as they thought dearest.
50.	With all the wealth of the world they dwelt there together

The most well-known knights under Christ himself,
And the loveliest ladies that ever had life,
And he the comeliest king that holds court;
For all this fair folk was in their first age,
55.   on the sill,
            The happiest under heaven,
            Their king the highest man of will;
            It were now great annoyance to name
            So hardy a host on any hill.

IV

60.   While New Year was so fresh that it was newly come,
        That day double on the dais was dinner served.
        When the king was come with knights into the hall,
        The chanting of the chapel achieved an end,
        Loud cries were cast there by clergy and others,
65.   Noel announced anew, named full oft;
        And then the rich ran forth to give presents,
        Cried year's gifts on high, gave them by hand,
        Debated busily about those gifts;
        Ladies laughed full loud, though they had lost,
70.   And he that won was not wroth, that you may well trust.
        All this mirth they made until mealtime;
        When they had washed worthily they went to sit,
        The best knight ever above, as it best seemed,
        Queen Guinevere, full gay, placed in the middle,
75.   Dressed on the dear dais, adorned all about,
        Fine silk beside her, a canopy over her
        Of tried Toulouse, of enough Tharsian tapestry,
        That were embroidered and inlaid with the best gems
        That might be proved worth its price with pennies to buy,
80.   any day.
            The comeliest to descry
            There glanced with eyes gray,
            A seemlier that he ever did espy
            Sooth might no man say.

V

85.   But Arthur would not eat til all were served,
        He was so joyous in his youth, and somewhat boyish:
        His life liked him light, he loved the less
        Either to long lie or to long sit,
        So busied him his young blood and his wild brain.
90.   And also another custom moved him so
        That through noblesse he had assumed, he would never eat
        Upon such a dear day ere him described were
        Of some adventurous thing an unknown tale
        Of some great marvel, that he might believe,
95.   Of elders, of arms, or other adventures,
        Or else some man besought him for some sure knight
        To join with him in jousting, in jeopardy to lay
        The man, life for life, each giving the other leave,
        As fortune would aid him, the fairer to have.
100.   This was the king's comportment when he was in court,
        At each pleasing feast among his free company
                in the hall.
            Therefore of face so fair
            He stands sturdy in stall,
105.   Full of vigor in that New Year
            Much mirth he makes with all.

VI

        Thus there stands in station the sturdy king himself
        Talking before the high table of trifles full pleasing.
        There good Gawain was placed beside Guinevere,
110.   And Agravain à la dure main on the other side sits,
        Both the king's sister's sons and full sure knights;
        Bishop Baldwin above begins the table,
        And Ywain, Urien's son, eats with him.
        They were arranged on the dais and there worthily served,
115.   And afterwards many sure men at the sideboards.

Then the first course came with blaring of trumpets,
With many a banner full bright that thereby hung;
New noise of nakers along with the noble pipes,
Wild warbles and boldly awakened sounds,
120.   That many a heart full high heaved at their touches.
Dainties went therewith of full dear meats,
An abundance of fresh foods, and on so many dishes
That it was difficult to find a place before the people
For to set the silverware that sundry stews held
125.   on the tablecloth.
            Each man as he loved himself
            There seized without loath;
            Every pair had dishes twelve,
            Good beer and bright wine both.

VII

130.   Now will I of their service say you no more;
For each wight may well know that there was no want there.
Another noise quite new drew quickly near
That the king might have leave to get some sustenance;
For scarcely was the noise not a while ceased,
135.   And the first course in the court kindly served,
There bursts in at the hall door a terrible lord,
The highest in measure on earth;
From the neck to the waist so square and so thick,
And his loins and his limbs so long and so great,
140.   Half giant on earth I suspect he was,
But of men by all means the most I recall him being,
And at that the merriest in his magnitude that might ride;
For though his back and his breast of his body were all stern,
Both his stomach and his waist were worthily small,
145.   And all his features proper, to the form he had,
                 full clean;
            For wonder of his hue men had,
            Set in his semblance as seen;

He strode in as a man bold,
150.   And overall dark green.

VIII

And all arrayed in green this man and his weeds:
A straight coat full strait, that stuck to his sides,
A merry mantle over that, adorned within
With fur trimmed plain, the lining full clean
155.   With blithe ermine full bright, and his hood the same,
That was loosed from his locks and laid on his shoulders;
Suitable well-drawn hose of that same hue,
Dispensed on his calf, and splendid spurs below
Of bright gold, upon silk borders barred full rich,
160.   And shoeless under shanks there the man rides;
And all his vesture verily was clean green,
Both the bars on his belt and other blithe stones,
That were richly arranged in his bright array
About himself and his saddle, upon silk works.
165.   That were too tedious to tell of half the trifles
That were embroidered therein, with birds and butterflies,
With gay gaudiness of green, the gold ever in the middle.
The pendants on his horse's breastplate, the proud crupper,
The bosses on the bit, and all the metal was enameled then,
170.   The stirrups that he stood in were stained the same,
And his saddle all after and his noble skirts,
That ever glimmered and gleamed of green stones;
The foal that he rides on fine of that ilk,
                    for certain.
175.   A green horse great and thick,
          A steed full stiff to restrain,
          In broad bridle quick;
          To the man he was fully suited.

IX

Full gay was this man attired in green,
180. And the hair of his head matched his horse.
Fair fanning locks cover his shoulders;
A large beard hangs over his breast like a bush,
That with the handsome hair that reaches out from his head
Was clipped all around above his elbows,
185. That half his arms thereunder were hidden in the fashion
Of a king's capados that encloses his neck;
The mane of that mighty horse was much to it like,
Well curled and combed, with knots full many
Folded in with a gold filament about the fair green,
190. Always one strand of the hair, another of gold;
The tail and the forelock plaited to suit,
And both bound with a band of bright green,
Decked with full dear stones, as long as the dock,
Then drawn tight by a thong with an intricate knot aloft,
195. There many bells full bright of burnished gold rung.
Such a horse upon earth, nor the knight that him rides,
Was never seen in that hall with sight ere that time,
           with eye.
         He looked as bright as lightning,
200.   So said all that did him sight;
         It seemed as if no man might
         Under his blows endure.

X

Yet he had no helm nor hauberk either,
Nor no chest armor, no plate appendant to arms,
205. Nor no shaft nor no shield to thrust or to smite,
But in his one hand he had a holly branch,
That is greatest in green when groves are bare,
And an axe in his other, huge and immense,
A battle-axe cruel to expound in words, whoso might.

210. The length of an ellwand the large head had,
     The spike all of green steel and hammered gold,
     The blade burnished bright, with a broad edge
     As well shaped to shear as sharp razors,
     The handle of a stiff staff the grim man gripped it by,
215. That was wound with iron to the weapon's end,
     And all engraved in green with gracious works;
     A thong wrapped about, that locked at the head,
     And so was fastened full oft round the stem,
     With choice tassels attached enough thereto
220. On buttons of bright green braid full rich.
     This knight hurtles himself in and the hall enters,
     Driving to the high dais, danger he feared not,
     Never one he hailed, but haughty he overlooked them.
     The first word that he offered, 'Where is,' he said,
225. 'The governor of this gang? Gladly I would
     See that man in sight, and with him speak
                         reason.'
                 On the knights he cast his eye
                 And rolled it up and down;
230.   He stopped and studied
                 Who there was most renowned.

XI

     There was looking at length the knight to behold,
     For each man had marveled what it might mean
     That a knight and a horse might assume such a hue
235. As to grow green as the grass and greener it seemed,
     Than green enamel glowing brighter on gold.
     All pondered that stood there, and stalked him near
     With all the wonder of the world as to what he would do.
     For many marvels had they seen, but such a one never;
240. Therefore for phantom and faery the folk there deemed it.

So many a noble knight was afraid to answer,
And all stunned at his voice sat stone-still
In a dead silence through the rich hall;
As if all were slipped into sleep so slackened their voices

245.   in height;
          I deem it not all out of fear,
          But some for courtesy,
          But let him whom all should revere
          Reckon with that wight.

XII

250.   Then Arthur before the high dais that adventure beholds,
        And rightly him reverenced, for afraid was he never,
        And said, 'Wight, welcome indeed to this place,
        The head of this hostel Arthur am I;
        Alight graciously and linger, I prithee,
255.   And whatsoever thy will is we shall learn after that.'
        'Nay, as he that sits on high help me,' quoth the knight,
        'To stay any while in this dwelling was not my errand;
        But the fame of thee, sir, is lifted up so high,
        And thy castle and thy men held as the best,
260.   Stoutest under steel-gear on steed to ride,
        The most valiant and the worthiest of the world's kind,
        Proven for to play with in other pure sports,
        And here is courtesy displayed, as I have heard say,
        And that has brought me hither, indeed, at this time.
265.   You may be assured by this branch that I bear here
        That I pass as in peace, and no plight seek;
        For had I fared in dress of fighting fashion,
        I have a hauberk at home and a helmet both,
        A shield and a sharp spear, shining bright,
270.   And other weapons to wield, I well imagine, also;
        But since I want no war, my weeds are softer.
        But if thou be so bold as all men tell,
        Thou will grant me gladly the game that I ask for

by right.'
275.   Arthur gave answer,
And said, 'Sir courteous knight,
If thou crave battle bare,
Here fail thou not a fight.'

XIII

'Nay, I ask no fight, in faith I tell thee,
280. There are about on this bench but beardless children.
If I were hasped in arms on a high steed,
Here is no man to match me, for their might so weak.
Therefore I crave in this court a Christmas game,
For it is Yule and New Year, and here are many daring men.
285. If any so hardy in this house holds himself,
Be so bold in his blood, so furious in his head,
That dare stoutly strike one stroke for another,
I shall give him as my gift this rich battle-axe,
This axe, that is heavy enough, to handle as he likes,
290. And I shall bide the first blow as bare as I sit.
If any man be so fell as to attempt what I tell,
Leap lightly toward me and seize this weapon,
I quitclaim it forever, keep it as his own,
And I shall stand him a stroke, steadfast on this floor,
295. Provided you grant me the right to deal him another
openly;
And yet give him respite
A twelve-month and a day;
Now hurry, and let us see
300.   If any herein dare aught say.'

XIV

If he astounded them at first, stiller were then
All the hired-men in the hall, the high and the low.

The man on his horse turned himself in his saddle,
And fiercely his red eyes he reeled about,
305.   Bent his bristled brows, brilliant green,
Waved his beard to wait for whoever would rise.
When none would keep discourse with him he coughed full loud,
And hemmed full richly, and prepared to speak:
'What, is this Arthur's house?' quoth the knight then,
310.   'All the fame of which runs through realms so many?
Where is now your arrogance and your conquests,
Your fierceness and your wrath, and your great words?
Now is the revelry and the renown of the Round Table
Overwhelmed with a word of one wight's speech,
315.   For all cower for fear without a blow shown!'
With this he laughs so loud that the lord grieved;
The blood shot for shame into his fair face
           and cheek;
       He waxed as wroth as the wind,
320.   So did all that were there.
       The king, keen in kind,
       Then stood near that stout man,

XV

And said, 'Knight, by heaven, your request is foolish,
And as thou hast asked for folly, it behooves thee to find it.
325.   I know no man that is aghast at thy great words,
Give now thy battle-axe, in God's name,
And I shall grant thee the boon that thou hast bode.'
Lightly he leaps toward him, and grasps at his hand,
Then fiercely that other man alights on foot.
330.   Now Arthur has the axe, and grips the handle,
And sternly stirs it about, his thought to strike with it.
The bold man stood before him tall,
Higher than any in the house by a head or more.
With stern expression there he stood and stroked his beard,
335.   And with a countenance unmoved he drew down his coat,

No more daunted nor dismayed at those mighty dints
Than if any man at the bench had brought him to drink
of wine.
Gawain, that sat by the queen,
340.   To the king he does incline:
'I beseech now with plain words
This melee may be mine.

XVI

'Would you, honorable lord,' quoth Gawain to the king,
'Bid me go from this bench, and stand by you there,
345.   That I without villainy might leave this table,
And if my liege lady be not displeased,
I would come to counsel you before your rich court.
For I think it not seemly, as is truly known,
When such an asking is raised so high in your hall,
350.   You yourself be inclined to take it upon yourself,
While many so bold about you sit on the bench
That under heaven I hope are none higher of will,
No better bodies on the field where fighting is reared.
I am the weakest, I wot, and of wit the feeblest,
355.   And my life the least loss, to tell the truth:
But for as much as you are my uncle am I only to be praised,
No bounty but your blood I in my body know;
And since this affair is so foolish that nought of it falls on you,
And I have asked you about it first, grant it to me;
360.   And if I speak unbecomingly, let all this rich court
be without blame.'
The nobles voiced together,
And since they all advised the same,
To release the king with crown
365.   And give Gawain the game.

XVII

Then commanded the king the knight for to rise;
And he full rapidly arose and approached him fair,
Kneeled down before the king, and seized that weapon;
And he granted it to him graciously, and lifted up his hand
370.   And gave him God's blessing, and gladly bids him
That his heart and his hand should both be hardy.
'Keep thee, cousin,' quoth the king, 'that thou be set on the cutting,
And if thou plan it right, truly I trow
That thou shall abide the blow that he shall bid after.'
375.   Gawain goes to the man with battle axe in hand,
And he boldly him abides, he was not the more abashed.
Then speaks to Sir Gawain the knight in the green,
'Reform we our contracts, before we go further.
First I entreat thee, knight, the name thou hast
380.   That thou tell me truly, that I may trust.'
'In good faith,' quoth the goodly knight, 'Gawain is my name,
That bids thee this buffet, whatsoever befalls after,
And at this time twelve months take from thee another
With whatever weapon thou wilt, and from no other wight
385.   on earth.'
        That other answered again,
        'Sir Gawain, so may I thrive,
        As I am extremely pleased
        At this dint that thou shall drive.

XVIII

390.   'By God,' quoth the green knight, 'Sir Gawain, me likes
That I shall get from your hand what I have asked for here.
And thou hast readily rehearsed, by reason full true,
Cleanly all the covenant that I asked of the king,
Save that thou shall assure me, man, by thy troth,
395.   That thou shall seek me thyself, wherever thou hope
I may be found on earth, and fetch thee such wages

As thou dealest me today before this rich nobility.'
'Where should I seek thee?' quoth Gawain, 'Where is thy place?
I wot not where thou dwelleth, by him who wrought me,

400. Nor do I know thee, knight, thy court nor thy name.
But teach me truly thereto, and tell me your name,
And I shall use all my wit to win me thither,
And that I swear thee forsooth, and by my sure troth.'
'That is enough at New Year, it needs no more,'

405. Quoth the man in green to Gawain the gracious
'If I tell thee truly when I have the tap,
And thou smoothly hath smitten me, smartly will I teach thee
Of my house and my home and my own name,
Then may thou question my conduct and hold to the contract;

410. And I expend no speech, then speed thou the better,
For thou may linger in thy land and seek no further —
but enough!
Take now thy grim tool to thee,
And let us see how thou knocks.'

415. 'Gladly, sir, forsooth,'
Quoth Gawain: his axe he strokes.

XIX

The green knight upon the ground readily arranges himself,
A little bow with the head, the flesh he uncovers,
His long lovely locks he laid over his crown,

420. Letting the naked neck show its note.
Gawain gripped the axe and gathers it on high,
The left foot on the floor he sets before him,
Lets the axe lightly alight on the naked flesh,
That the sharp blade shattered the bones of the man,

425. And sunk through the sheer flesh, and severed it in two,
That the blade of the burnished steel bit into the ground,
The fair head from the neck hit to the earth,
That many kicked it with their feet, there it forth rolled;
The blood spurted from the body, it gleamed on the green;

430. And neither faltered nor fell the man nevertheless,
     But stoutly he started forth upon stiff shanks,
     And roughly he reached out, there as the knights stood,
     Laid hold of his lovely head, and lifted it up at once;
     And then goes to his steed, the bridle he catches,
435. Steps into stirrups and strides aloft,
     And his head by the hair in his hand holds.
     And as steadfastly the man in his saddle sat
     As if no mishap had ailed him, though headless he were
                         in that stead.
440.   He twisted his bulk about,
              That ugly body that bled;
              Many of them were afraid
              By the time his reasons were read.

XX

     For the head in his hand he holds up even,
445. Towards the dearest on the dais he addresses the face,
     And it lifted up the eyelids and looked full broad,
     And spoke thus much with his mouth, as ye may now hear:
     'Look, Gawain, that thou be ready to go as thou promised,
     And search as faithfully til thou me, sir, find
450. As thou hath sworn in this hall, in hearing of these knights;
     To the Green Chapel thou proceed, I charge thee, to get
     Such a dint as thou hast dealt, hast deserved,
     To be readily given on New Year's morn.
     As The Knight of the Green Chapel many men know me,
455. Therefore if thou ask to find me, never shalt thou fail.
     Therefore, come, else thou deserve to be called recreant.'
     With a violent roar the reins he turns,
     Hastened out at the hall door, his head in his hand,
     That the fire of the flint flew from the foal's hooves.
460. To what land he went none there knew,
     No more than they wist from whence he was come.

What then?
The king and Gawain there
At the green man they laugh and grin;
465.   Yet it was noted full bare
A marvel among those men.

XXI

Though Arthur the gracious king wondered at heart,
He let no semblance be seen, but said full loud
To the comely queen with courteous speech,
470.   'Dear dame, let nothing you dismay today;
Well becomes such craft upon Christmas,
Playing of interludes, to laugh and to sing,
Among these kindly carols of knights and ladies.
Nevertheless to my meat I may me well repair,
475.   For I have seen a marvel I may not deny.'
He glanced upon Sir Gawain, and gainly he said,
'Now sir, hang up thy axe, that has hewn enough.'
And it was put above the dais on the dossal to hang,
There all men for marvel might on it look,
480.   And by true token thereof tell of its wonder.
Then they went to a table, these knights together,
The king and the good knight, and keen men served them
Of all dainties double, as might fall to the dearest;
With all manner of meat and minstrelsy both,
485.   With delight they spent that day, til daylight's end
in the land.
Now think well, Sir Gawain,
For danger that thou not shrink
This adventure for to seek
490.   That thou hast taken in hand.

FITT 2

I

This handsel of adventure has Arthur as first
In the young year, for he yearned to hear boasting.
Though words were wanting him when they went to sit,
Now are they stocked with stern work, staffed-full their hands.
495.   Gawain was glad to begin those games in the hall,
But though the end be heavy have ye no wonder;
For though men be merry when they have strong drink,
A year speeds full fast, and never yields the like,
The formation to the finish unfolds full seldom.
500.   Therefore this Yule went by, and the year after,
And each season ensued after the other:
After Christmas came the crabbed Lenten
That tries the flesh with fish and food more simple;
But then the weather of the world with winter it contests,
505.   Cold clings down, clouds uplift,
Sheer sheds the rain in showers full warm,
Falls upon the air plain, flowers there showing,
Both grounds and groves green are their garments,

Birds bustle to build, and furiously sing
510.   For joy of the soft summer that ensues
on the bank;
And blossoms swell to bloom
By hedgerows rich and rank,
Then notes noble enough
515.   Are heard in woods so splendid.

II

After the season of summer with the soft winds,
When Zephyrus softly blows on seeds and herbs,
Very fine is the growth that waxes thereout,
When the moistening dew drops from the leaves,
520.   To bide a blissful blush of the bright sun.
But then hastens the harvest, and hardens it at once,
Warns it for the winter to wax full ripe.
He drives with drought the dust for to rise
From the face of the earth to fly full high;
525.   Wrathful wind of the welkin wrestles with the sun,
Leaves launch from the lindens and alight on the ground,
And all gray the grass that green was ere.
Then all ripens and rots that first rose up,
And thus passes the year in many yesterdays,
530.   And winter returns, as the world demands,
in fact;
Til Michaelmas moon
Was come with winter's pledge;
Then thinks Gawain right quickly
535.   Of his anxious voyage.

III

Yet til All Hallows' Day with Arthur he lingers;
And he made a feast on that holiday for the knight's sake,

With much revelry and richness of the Round Table.
Knights full courteous and comely ladies
540. All for love of that man in longing they were,
But nevertheless they mentioned only mirth;
Many joyless for that gentleman made jests there.
And after meat with mourning he addresses his uncle,
And speaks of his passage, and plainly he said,
545. 'Now, liege lord of my life, I ask you leave;
You know the cost of this case, I care no more
To tell you the troubles thereof, naught but a trifle;
But I am setting out tomorrow without fail for the blow
To seek the man in green, as God will guide me.'
550. Then the best in the burg bowed together,
Ywain and Eric, and others full many,
Sir Dodinal le Savage, the Duke of Clarence,
Lancelot and Lionel, and Lucan the good,
Sir Bors and Sir Bedivere, big men both,
555. And many other nobles, with Mador de la Port.
All this company of court came near the king
For to counsel the knight, with care in their heart.
There was much dear dolor felt in the hall
That one so worthy as Gawain should wend on that errand,
560. To endure a doleful dint, and deal no more
                      with blade.
              The knight was always of good cheer,
              And said, 'What should I fear?
              Of destinies harsh or dear
565.   What may a man do but try?'

IV

He dawdles there all that day, and dresses on the morn,
Asks early for his arms, and they were all brought.
First a silken carpet was spread on the floor,
And much was the golden gear that gleamed therealoft.
570. The stout man steps thereon, and handles the steel,

Dressed in a doublet of dear Tharsian silk,
And after that a crafty capados, closed aloft,
That with a bright ermine was bounded within.
Then set they the sabatons upon the man's feet,
575. His legs lapped in steel with lovely greaves,
With polains pitched thereto, polished full clean,
About his knees attached with knots of gold;
Neat cuisses then, that cunningly enclosed
His thick thewed thighs, with thongs attached thereto;
580. And then the braided byrnie of bright steel rings
Upon fine stuff enveloped that wight,
And well burnished braces upon both his arms,
With elbow guards good and gay, and gloves of steel plate,
And all the goodly gear that should be his gain
585.   at the time;
             With rich coat-armor
             His gold spurs employed with pride,
             Girt with a sword full sure
             With a silk sash about his side.

V

590. When he was hasped in arms, his harness was rich:
The least latchet or loop shone of gold.
So harnessed as he was he hearkened to his mass,
Offered and honored at the high altar.
Then he came to the king and to his court-company,
595. Graciously takes his leave of lords and ladies;
And they him kissed and conveyed, commending him to Christ.
By that time Gringolet was ready, and girt with a saddle
That gleamed full gaily with many gold fringes,
Everywhere studded full new, for that purpose intended;
600. The bridle barred about, with bright gold bound,
The apparel of the poitrel and of the proud skirts,
The crupper and the caparison accorded with the saddle bows;
And all was arrayed on red rich gold nails,

So that all glittered and glinted as the gleam of the sun.
605. Then seizes he his helmet, and hastily it kisses,
That was stiffly stapled and stuffed within.
It was high on his head, hasped behind,
With a light covering over the ventail,
Embroidered and bound with the best gems
610. On a broad silk border and birds on the seams,
As popinjays painted preening between,
Turtledoves and true lovers entwined so thick
As if many maids had worked on it for seven winters
                    in town.
615.   The circlet was of more price
                That clipped round his crown,
                Diamonds of the best
                That were both bright and brown.

VI

Then they showed him the shield, that was of sheer gules,
620. With the pentangle painted of pure gold hues.
He brandished it by the baldric, about his neck casts it,
That became the man seemingly fair.
And why the pentangle appends to that noble prince
I intend to tell you, though it should delay me:
625. It is a sign that Solomon set some time
In betokening of troth, by the title that it has,
For it is a figure that holds five points,
And each line overlaps and locks in the other,
And everywhere it is endless; and the English call it
630. Overall, as I hear, the endless knot.
Therefore it accords with this knight and his clear arms,
For ever faithful in five and in five separate ways
Gawain was for good known, and as gold refined,
Devoid of each villainy, with virtues adorned
635.   at court;
                Therefore the pentangle new

He bore on shield and coat;
As man of word most true
And gentlest knight of speech.

VII

640.   First he was found faultless in his five wits,
And next failed never the knight in his five fingers,
And all his affiance on earth was in the five wounds
That Christ caught on the cross, as the creed tells;
And wheresoever this man in the melee was stood,
645.   His thorough thought was on this, through all other things,
That all his courage he derived from the five joys
That the gracious heaven-queen had of her child;
This caused the comely knight to have
In the inner half of his shield her image depicted,
650.   So that when he looked thereto his heart never lessened.
The fifth five that I find the man used
Was franchise and fellowship before all things,
His purity and his courtesy were never crooked,
And piety, that passeth all points: these pure five
655.   Were harder laid on the man than on any other.
Now all these five things, forsooth, were fastened on this knight,
And each one linked with the other, that none had an end,
And fixed upon five points, that failed never,
Nor came together in no direction, nor sundered neither,
660.   Without ending at any angle anywhere I find,
Wherever the process began or came to an end.
Therefore on his shiny shield shaped was the knot
Royally with red gold upon red gules,
That is the pure pentangle called so by the people
665.   with lore.
Now prepared is Gawain gay,
And seized his lance right there,
And bade them all good day,
He thought for evermore.

VIII

670. He strikes the steed with the spurs and sprang on his way,
So strongly that the stone-fire flashed out thereafter
All that saw that seemly one were sick at heart,
And said the same men softly all together to each other,
Caring for that comely one, 'By Christ, it is a shame
675. That thou, lord, shall be lost, that art of noble life!
To find his equal upon earth, in faith, is not easy.
To have acted more carefully would have been wiser,
And worth it to have made yonder dear man a duke;
A laudable leader of men in the land he well would seem,
680. And so had better have been than battered to naught,
Beheaded by an elvish man, for unguarded pride.
Whoever knew any king such counsel to take
As knights a-cavilling at Christmas games!'
Very much was the warm water welling from eyes
685. When that seemly sire set out from the dwelling
           that day.
      He made no abode,
      But swiftly went his way;
      Many winding ways he rode,
690.   As I heard the book say.

IX

Now rides this knight through the realm of Logres,
Sir Gawain, in God's name, though he thought it no game.
Oft friendless and alone he lodges at night
Where he found not before him the fare that he liked.
695. He had no company but his horse by forest and hill,
Nor anyone but God to speak with along the way,
Til that he came full nigh into North Wales.
All the isles of Anglesy on his left he holds,
And fares over the fords by the forelands,
700. Over at the Holy Head, til he had the high ground

In the wilderness of Wirral; wandered there but few
That either God or man with good heart loved.
And always he asked as he fared, of men that he met,
If they had heard any word of a green knight,
705.   In any ground thereabout, of the green chapel;
And all answered him with nay, that never in their life
Had they seen a man that was of such hue
of green.
The knight took ways strange
710.   Along many a rugged slope,
His cheer full oft showed change
That chapel ere he might see.

X

Many cliffs he climbed over in countries strange,
Far flung from his friends foreignly he rides.
715.   At each strand on stream where the wight passed
He found a foe before him, unless a wonder it were,
And one so foul and so fell that it behooved him to fight.
So many marvels by the hills there the man finds,
It were too tedious to tell of the tenth part.
720.   Sometimes with wyrms he wars, and with wolves also,
Sometimes with wood-trolls that dwelt in the crags,
Both with bulls and bears, and boars at other times,
And ogres that panted after him of the high fells.
Had he not been doughty and duty-bound, and had served the Lord,
725.   Doubtless he had been dead and dashed full oft.
For warring bothered him not so much that winter was not worse,
When the cold clear water from the clouds shed,
And froze ere it might fall to the fallow earth.
Near slain with the sleet he slept in his armor
730.   More nights than enough in naked rocks,
There as clattering from the crest the cold stream runs,
And hanged high over his head in hard icicles.
Thus in peril and pain and plights full hard

Cross country rides this knight, til Christmas even,
735.   alone;
           The knight well that tide,
           To Mary made his moan,
           That she would advise him to ride
           And guide him to some abode.

XI

740.   By a mountain on the morn merrily he rides
       Into a forest full deep, that was wondrously wild;
       High hills on each side, and woods below
       Of hoary oaks full huge a hundred together;
       The hazel and the hawthorn were all entangled,
745.   With rough ragged moss arrayed everywhere,
       With many unblithe birds upon bare twigs,
       That piteously piped there for pain of the cold.
       The man upon Gringolet glides under them,
       Through many a marsh and mire, a man all alone,
750.   Concerned for his circumstances, lest he should not survive
       To see the service of that sire, that on that same night
       Of a maid was born, our sorrow to quell.
       And therefore sighing he said, 'I beseech thee, lord,
       And Mary, that is mildest mother so dear,
755.   Of some harbor where highly I might hear mass,
       And thy matins tomorrow, meekly I ask,
       And thereto promptly I pray my pater and ave
                        and creed.'
           He rode as he prayed,
760.   And cried for his misdeeds,
           He crossed himself many times,
           And said, 'Christ's Cross speed me!'

XII

He, the man, had crossed himself but thrice
Ere he was aware in the wood of an abode on a hill,
765.   Above a glade, on a mound, locked under boughs
Of many burly boles about by the ditches:
A castle the comeliest that ever knight owned,
Pitched on a prairie, a park all about,
With a piked palisade pinned full thick,
770.   That embraced many trees for more than two miles.
That stronghold on that one side the knight viewed
As it shimmered and shone through the sheer oaks;
Then he graciously takes off his helmet, and highly he thanks
Jesus and Saint Julian, that gentle are both,
775.   That accorded him courtesy, and his cry hearkened.
'Now good hostel,' quoth the man, 'I beseech you yet!'
Then he goads Gringolet with his gilt heels,
And fully by chance he hath chosen the chief gateway,
That clearly brought the man to the bridge end
780.   in haste.
        The bridge was clearly upraised,
        The gates were shut fast,
        The walls were well arrayed,
        They feared no wind's blast.

XIII

785.   The knight sat on the steed, that tarried on the bank
Of the deep double ditch that drove to the place;
The wall waded in the water wondrously deep,
And again a full huge height it hailed aloft
Of hard hewn stone up to the cornice,
790.   Buttressed under the battlement in the best way;
And then turrets full gay placed between,
With many lovely loopholes that locked full clean:
A better barbican that man glanced upon never.

And innermore he beheld that hall full high,
795.　Towers set up between, furnished full thick,
　　　Fair finials that fitted, and wonderfully long,
　　　With carved capstones craftily constructed.
　　　Chalk-white chimneys there he perceived enough
　　　Upon bastion roofs, that gleamed full white;
800.　So many painted pinnacles were peppered everywhere,
　　　Among the castle crenels clambered so thick
　　　That pared out of paper purely it seemed.
　　　The noble knight on the steed thought it fair enough,
　　　If he might manage to come within the cloister,
805.　To harbor in that hostel while the holy day lasted,
　　　　　　　　conveniently.
　　　　　　He called, and soon there came
　　　　　　A porter pure pleasant,
　　　　　　On the wall his errand he takes,
810.　　　　And hailed the knight errant.

XIV

　　　'Good sir,' quoth Gawain, 'would thou go with my message
　　　To the high lord of this house, harbor to crave?'
　　　'Yes, by Peter,' quoth the porter, 'and I truly believe
　　　That ye be, wight, welcome to dwell while you like.'
815.　Then went that wight quickly and came again at once,
　　　And pleasant folk with him, to welcome the knight.
　　　They let down the great drawbridge and dearly went out,
　　　And kneeled down on their knees upon the cold earth
　　　To welcome this same wight as they thought him worthy;
820.　They yielded him the broad gate, jerked up wide,
　　　And he promptly bade them rise, and rode over the bridge.
　　　Several men seized him by the saddle, while he alighted,
　　　And the men stout enough stabled his steed.
　　　Knights and squires came down then
825.　For to bring this man into the hall with bliss;
　　　When he hefted up his helmet, there hied enough

For to take it at his hand, the gentleman to serve;
His sword and his shield both they took.
Then greeted he full graciously those nobles each one,
830. And many proud men pressed forward there that prince to honor.
All hasped in his high weeds to the hall they led him,
Where a fair fire upon the floor fiercely burned.
Then the lord of the people came down from his chamber
For to meet with honor the man on the floor;
835. He said, 'Ye are welcome to do as you like
With what here is: all is your own, to have at your will
                    and wielding.'
              'Grant mercy,' quoth Gawain,
              'There may Christ repay it you.'
840.   As men seeming glad
              Each embraced the other in his arms.

XV

Gawain glanced at the man that greeted him goodly,
And thought him a bold knight that owned the burg;
A huge knight indeed, and in the prime of life;
845. Broad, bright, was his beard, and all beaver-hued,
Stern, sturdy in striding on stalwart shanks,
Fell face as the fire, and free of his speech,
And well it suited him, forsooth, as the man thought,
To lead a lordship in the shelter of full good company.
850. The lord conveyed him to a chamber, and chiefly commands
To deliver him a man, him humbly to serve;
And there were ready at his bidding enough men,
That brought him to a bright bower, where bedding was noble,
Curtains of clear silk with clear gold hems,
855. And coverlets full curious with comely panels
Of bright ermine above, embroidered at the sides,
Curtains running on ropes, red gold rings,
Tapestries tight to the wall of Toulouse and Tharsia,
And underfoot on the floor, following suit.

860. There he was despoiled, with speech of mirth,
     The man of his byrnie and of his bright weeds.
     Rich robes full readily men brought him,
     For to take and to change, and choose of the best.
     As soon as he donned one and was dressed therein,
865. That sat on him seemly with sailing skirts,
     Vernal by his visage verily it seemed
     Well-nigh to each man, all in hues
     Glowing and lovely all his limbs under,
     That a comelier knight Christ never made,
870.   thought they.
                   From whence in the world he were,
                   It seemed as he might
                   Be a prince without peer
                   In the field where fell men fought.

XVI

875. A chair before the chimney, where charcoal burned,
     Was readied for Sir Gawain readily with cloths,
     Cushions upon quilted coverlets that were both quaint;
     And then a merry mantle was on that man cast
     Of a brown blend, embroidered full rich
880. And fair furred within with pelt of the best,
     All of ermine on earth, his hood of the same;
     And he sat in that seat seemly rich,
     And he warmed himself chiefly, and then his cheer mended.
     Soon was set up a table on trestles full fair,
885. Clad with a clean cloth that clear white showed,
     Surnape, and salt cellar, and silver spoons.
     The wight washed at his will and went to his meat:
     Men served him seemly enough,
     With several and suitable soups, seasoned of the best,
890. Double-fold, as is fitting, and many kinds of fish,
     Some baked in bread, some broiled on the coals,
     Some seethed, some in stew savored with spices,

And always sauces so subtle that the man liked.
The knight called it a feast full freely and oft
895. Full graciously, when all the noblemen confronted him at once,
as gracious,
'This penance now ye take,
And soon it shall amend.'
That man much mirth can make,
900. For the wine to his head did wend.

XVI

Then was searched and enquired for in a careful way
By privy points of that prince, put to himself,
So that he confessed courteously to be of the court
That noble Arthur the gracious one holds alone,
905. That is the rich royal king of the Round Table,
And it was Gawain himself that was sitting in that dwelling,
Come that Christmas, as the case befell him then.
When the lord learned that he had the man there,
Loud laughed he thereat, so pleasing he thought it,
910. And all the men in that castle made much joy
To appear in his presence at expressly that time,
That all value and prowess and refined virtue
Appends to his person, and praised is ever;
Before all men on earth his honor is the highest.
915. Each man full softly said to his companion:
'Now we shall properly see patterns of virtue
And the spotless terms of noble talking,
What speeds in speech we may learn unspurred,
Since we have procured this fine father of nurture.
920. God has given us his goodly grace forsooth,
That such a guest as Gawain grants us to have,
When men blithely of his birth shall sit
and sing.
To the meaning of manners sheer
925. This man now shall us bring,

I hope those who may him hear
Shall learn of love-talking.'

XVII

When dinner was done and the dear one risen
It was near the time when night drew nigh.
930. Chaplains to the chapels had chosen the way,
Rang the bells full richly, as they should,
For the devout evensong of the high season.
The lord departs thereto, and the lady also,
Into a comely closet quaintly she enters.
935. Gawain glides full gay and goes thither at once;
The lord seizes him by the sleeve and leads him to a seat,
And knows him familiarly and calls him by name,
And said he was the most welcome wight in the world;
And he thanked him thoroughly, and each clasped the other,
940. And sat soberly together during the service.
Then list the lady to look on the knight,
Then came she out of her closet with many comely maids.
She was the fairest in skin, of flesh and of muscle,
And of compass and color and manners, of all others,
945. And finer than Guinevere, as the wight thought.
She chased through the chancel to cherish that nobleman:
Another lady led her by the left hand,
That was older than she, an ancient it seemed,
And highly honored with knights about.
950. But those ladies were unlike to look upon,
For if the young one was fresh, yellow was the other;
Rich red on that one was arrayed everywhere,
Rough wrinkled cheeks rolled on that other one;
Kerchiefs of that one, with many clear pearls,
955. Her breast and her bright throat bare displayed,
Shone sheerer than snow that sheds on hills;
That other with a gorget over her neck was attired,
Bundled over her black chin with chalk-white veils,

Her front enfolded in silk, muffled up everywhere,
960.   Turreted and trellised with trifles about,
That naught was bare of that lady but the black brows,
The two eyes and the nose, the naked lips,
And those were sour to see and strangely bleared;
A worshipped lady of the world one might call her,
965.   by God!
            Her body was short and thick,
            Her buttocks bulging and broad,
            More delectable to look upon
            Was the one that she led.

XVIII

970.   When Gawain glanced at that gay one, that looked back graciously,
With leave left of the lord he went again to them;
The elder he greeted, bowing full low,
The lovelier he laps a little in his arms,
He kisses her sweetly and knightly he speaks.
975.   They request acquaintance of him, and he quickly asks
To be their servant soothly, if they liked.
They took him between them, with talking led him
To chamber, to chimney, and chiefly they request
Spices, that men speeded to bring them unsparingly,
980.   And winning wine therewith each time.
The lord lovely aloft leaps full oft,
Minded to have mirth be made many times,
Nobly removed his hood, hung it on a spear,
And offered them to win the worship thereof,
985.   That most mirth might move that Christmas while:
'And I shall try, by my faith, to strive with the best
Ere I lose my garment, with the help of my friends.'
Thus with laughing words the lord makes merry
For to gladden Sir Gawain with games in the hall
990.   that night,

Til that it was time
The lord commanded light;
Sir Gawain his leave could take
And to his bed he went.

XIX

995.   On the morn, as each man remembers that time
When God for our destiny today was born,
Weal waxed in each dwelling in the world for his sake;
So it did there on that day through many dainties.
Both at mess and at meal dishes full quaint
1000. Brave men served upon the dais dressed of the best.
The old ancient woman in the highest place sits,
The lord politely beside her, as I believe;
Gawain and the gay lady together they sat,
Even in the middle, where the mess meetly came,
1005. And then through all the hall as best suited them.
By the time each man was properly served according to his degree,
There was meat, there was mirth, there was much joy,
That for me to tell thereof it were troublesome,
And to pinpoint it yet would pain me peradventure.
1010. But yet I know that Gawain and the noble lady
Such comfort of their company attained together
Through the dear dalliance of their secret words,
With clean courteous talk free from filth,
That their play surpassed any princely game
1015.   verily.
                Trumpets and nakers,
                Much piping resided there;
                Each man tended his,
1019.   And those two tended theirs.

XX

1020. Much delight was derived there that day and the next,
      And the third as thoroughly thronged in thereafter;
      The joy of Saint John's Day was glorious to hear,
      And was the last of the like, people there thought.
      There were guests going upon the gray morn,
1025. Therefore wondrously they stayed awake, and drank the wine,
      Danced the full duration with dear carols.
      At last, when it was late, they took their leave,
      Each one to wend on his way that was a stranger.
      Gawain bids him good day, the good man seizes him,
1030. Leads him to his own chamber, beside the chimney,
      And there he delays him, and dearly thanks him
      For the fine favor that he had done him
      By honoring his house on that high tide,
      And embellishing his castle with his fine cheer.
1035. 'Indeed, sir, while I live, my worth is better
      That Gawain has been my guest at God's own feast.'
      'Gramercy, sir,' quoth Gawain, 'in good faith it is yours,
      All the honor is your own — may the high king repay you!
      And I am a wight at your will to work at your behest,
1040. As I am held thereto, in high and in low,
                 by right.'
           The lord takes many pains
           To hold longer the knight;
           To him answers Gawain
1045.   There is no way that he might.

XXI

      Then the lord inquired full fair of him
      What daring deed had driven him at that dear time
      So keenly from the king's court to proceed all alone
      Ere the holidays were wholly over in town.
1050. 'Forsooth, sir,' quoth the man, 'ye say but the truth,

A high errand and a hasty one drove me from home,
For I am summoned myself to seek such a place,
I know not in the world whitherward to wend to find it.
I would not miss being near it on New Year's morn
1055. For all the land in Logres, so help me our lord!
Therefore, sir, this inquest I require of you here,
That ye tell me truthfully if ye ever heard tale
Of the green chapel, where it stands upon earth,
And of the knight that keeps it, of color of green.
1060. There was established by statute an appointment between us,
To meet that man at that spot, if I might last;
And of that same New Year but little now remains,
And I would look on that man, if God would let me,
More gladly, by God's son, than possess any good!
1065. Therefore, indeed, by your will, it behooves me to go,
I have now for business but barely three days,
And I would as fain fall dead as fail of my errand.'
Then laughing quoth the lord, 'Now it behooves thee to stay,
For I shall teach you those terms by the time's end,
1070. Let the green chapel's ground grieve you no more;
But you shall be in your bed, sir, at thine ease,
While forth is day, and fare on the first of the year,
And come to that mark at mid-morn, to do what you like
                              in expense.
1075.   Dwell til New Year's day,
                 And rise, and journey then,
                 Someone shall set you on the way,
                 It is not two miles hence.'

XXII

Then was Gawain full glad, and gamely he laughed:
1080. 'Now I thank you thrivingly throughout all other things,
Now achieved is my chance, I shall at your will
Dwell, and do what else you deem.'
Then the sire seized him and set him by his side,

Letting the ladies be fetched to please them the better.
1085. There was seemly solace by themselves silent;
The lord out of love uttered words so merry
As a wight out of his wits would, not knowing what he might.
Then he said to the knight, crying loudly,
'Ye have deemed to do the deed that I bid;
1090. Will you hold to this behest here at this instant?'
'Yes, sir, forsooth,' said the knight true,
'While I bide in your burg, be obedient to your behest.'
'For ye have traveled,' quoth the man, 'drawn from faraway,
And then stayed awake with me, you are not well recovered
1095. Neither of sustenance nor of sleep, soothly I know;
Ye shall linger in your loft, and lie at your ease
Tomorrow until mass-time, and to meat wend
When ye will, with my wife, that with you shall sit
And comfort you with company, til I return to court;
1100.   you stay,
              And I shall early rise,
              On hunting will I go.'
              Gawain grants all this,
              Bowing, as the courteous one he is.

XXIII

1105. 'Yet further,' quoth the man, 'a covenant let us make:
Whatsoever I win in the wood becomes yours
And whatever check you may receive exchange it with me.
Good sir, let us swap so, swear with truth,
Whether, man, something befalls, worthless or better.'
1110. 'By God,' quoth Gawain the good, 'I agree thereto,
And whatever you list to like is pleasing to me.'
'Bring us beverage, and this bargain is made':
So said the lord of that people; they laughed each one,
They drank and dallied and dealt in revelry,
1115. These lords and ladies, as long as they pleased:
And then with Frankish behavior and many fair words

They stood and stopped and quietly spoke,
Kissed full sweetly and took their leave.
With many servants full swift and gleaming torches
1120. Each man to his bed was brought at last,
                    full soft.
            To bed yet ere they went,
            The terms were recorded oft;
            The old lord of that people
1125.   Could well hold the fun aloft.

FITT 3

I

        Full early before the day the folk arose,
        Guests that wanted to go called their grooms,
        And they hurried up in haste, horses to saddle,
        Tying down their tackle, trussing their bags,
1130.   The richest enrich themselves, to ride all arrayed,
        Leap up lightly, seize their bridles,
        Each wight on his way wherever he well liked.
        The loving lord of the land was not the last
        Arrayed for the riding, with men full many;
1135.   He ate a sop hastily, when he had heard mass,
        With bugle to hunting field he hurried in haste,
        So that by the time any daylight shone upon earth
        He with his knights on high horses were.
        Then these catchers that could coupled their hounds,
1140.   Unclosed the kennel door and called them thereout,
        Blew bigly in bugles three bare notes;
        Brachs bayed therefor and made fierce noise;

And they chastised and chided those that went on chasing,
A hundred hunters, as I have heard tell,
1145.   of the best.
               To hunting stations keepers went,
               Huntsmen cast off couples;
               There rose for a good blast
               Great uproar in that forest.

II

1150. At the first cry of the quest the wild creatures quaked;
       Deer drove in the dale, foolish with fear,
       Hurried to the height, but fiercely they were
       Turned back by the beaters, that stoutly shouted.
       They let the harts have the path, with their high heads,
1155. The rugged bucks also with their broad antlers;
       For the free lord had forbidden in the closed season
       That any man should meddle with the male deer.
       The hinds were held with hey! and ware!
       The does driven with great din to the deep glades.
1160. There one might see, as they slipped, slanting of arrows —
       At each wend in the wood whopped an arrow —
       That deeply bit into the brown hide with full broad heads.
       What! they bray and bleed, on the slopes they die,
       And always hounds in a rush swiftly followed them,
1165. Hunters with loud horns hastened after them
       With such a cracking cry as if cliffs had burst.
       Whatever wild animal escaped the men's shots
       Was all torn and rent at the receiving station,
       By the time they were harassed at the height and chased to the waters;
1170. The men were so learned at the lower stations,
       And the greyhounds so great, that they seized them at once
       And tore them down, as fast as men might look,
                   right there.
               The lord for bliss emboldened
1175.   Full oft can lance and alight;

And drove that day with joy
Thus til the dark night.

III

Thus sports the lord by the linden's edge,
And Gawain the good man in gay bed lies,
1180.   Lurks while the daylight gleamed on the walls,
Under coverlet full fair, curtained about;
And as in slumber he slid, slyly he heard
A little din at his door, and stealthily open;
And he heaved up his head out of his clothes,
1185.   A corner of the curtain he caught up a little,
And waits warily thitherward to see what it might be.
It was the lady, loveliest to behold,
That drew the door after her full secretly and silently,
And bent toward the bed; and the man was ashamed,
1190.   And laid him down cunningly and let on as if he slept;
And she stepped stilly and stole to his bed,
Cast up the curtain and crept within,
And seated herself full softly on the bed-side,
And lingered there strangely long to look when he wakened.
1195.   The man lay lurking a full long while,
Compassed in his conscience as to what the case might
Promote or amount — a marvel he thought,
But yet he said to himself, 'More seemly it were
To espy with my speech at once what she wants.'
1200.   Then he wakened, and stretched, and turned toward her,
And unlocked his eyelids, and acted surprised,
And crossed himself, as by his saying the safer to become,
                    by hand.
                With chin and cheek full sweet,
1205.   Both white and red in blend,
                Full lovely did she speak
                With small laughing lips.

IV

'Good morning, Sir Gawain,' said that gay lady,
'Ye are a sleeper unsly, that one may slide hither;
1210.   Now ye are taken straightaway! Unless a truce we may shape,
I shall bind you in your bed, be sure of that.'
All laughing the lady uttered these jests.
'Good morning, gay lady,' quoth Gawain the blithe,
'I shall do as you will, and that likes me well,
1215.   For I surrender quickly, and beg for mercy,
And that is best, in my judgment, for I needs must':
And thus he jested in return with much blithe laughter.
'But would ye, lady lovely, then grant me leave,
And release your prisoner, and pray him to rise,
1220.   I would be out of this bed, and be better dressed,
I should have the more comfort to discourse with you.'
'Nay, forsooth, good sir,' said that sweet lady,
'Ye shall not rise from your bed, I intend better for you.
I shall wrap you here, that other half also,
1225.   And then converse with the knight that I have caught;
For I know well, indeed, ye are Sir Gawain,
That all the world worships wheresoever ye ride;
Your honor, your courtesy is courteously praised
By lords, by ladies, by all that bear life.
1230.   And now ye are here, indeed, and we both are one;
My lord and his men are gone faraway,
Other men in their beds, and my women also,
The door drawn and locked with a doughty hasp;
And since I have in this house him that all like,
1235.   I shall spend my time well, while it lasts,
             with talk.
         Ye are welcome to my body,
         Your own wants to choose,
         Sheer necessity behooves me
1240.   Your servant to be, and I shall.

V

'In good faith,' quoth Gawain, 'a gain it me thinketh
Though I be not he of whom ye have spoken;
To attain such reverence as ye rehearse here
I am a wight unworthy, I wot well myself.
1245. By God, I were glad, if you thought it good,
That in word or deed I might arrange
For the pleasure of your praise — it were a pure joy.'
'In good faith, Sir Gawain,' quoth the gay lady,
The praise and the prowess that pleases all others,
1250. If I found it lacking or lightsome, it were hardly dainty;
But there are ladies enough that now would rather
Have thee, noble one, in their hold, as I have thee here,
To dally with dearly your dainty words,
Offer them comfort and kill their cares,
1255. Than much of the treasure or gold that they have.
But I love that same lord that holds up the heavens,
I have it wholly in my hand that which all desire,
                    through grace.'
                She gave him such great cheer,
1260.   That was so fair of face,
                The knight with speeches pure
                Answered each single case.

VI

'Madame,' quoth the merry man, 'May Mary repay you,
For I have found, in good faith, your frankness noble,
1265. And others receive full much for their deeds from other folk,
But the delight they deal is not even my desert,
It is the worship of yourself, that know naught but good.'
'By Mary,' said the honorable one, 'I think otherwise;
For were I worth all the sum of women alive,
1270. And all the wealth of the world were in my hands,
And I could shop and choose to find me a lord,

For the qualities I have recognized in thee, knight, here
Of beauty and debonairness and blithe semblance,
And that I have hearkened ere and beheld here as true,
1275. There should be no man on earth chosen before you.'
'Indeed, worthy lady,' quoth the wight, 'ye have chosen much better,
But I am proud of the praise that ye put on me,
And soberly your servant, my sovereign I hold you,
And your knight I become, and may Christ reward you.'
1280. Thus they spoke of many things til past midmorn,
And always the lady acted like she loved him much.
The man fared with defense and entertained full fair;
Though she was the most splendid lady the man could imagine,
The less love in his course of ruin he sought
1285.   without delay —
        The dint that should be dealt him,
        And needs it must be done.
        The lady then spoke of leave,
        He granted it her full soon.

VII

1290. Then she bade him good day, and with a glance laughed,
And as she stood, she astounded him with a full store of words:
'Now he that speeds each speech reward you for this disport!
But that ye be Gawain, my mind questions it.'
'Wherefore?' quoth the man, and freshly he asks,
1295. Fearing lest he had failed in form of his caste;
But the lady blessed him, and 'For this reason' said:
'As good as Gawain gainly is held to be,
And courtesy is enclosed so clean in himself,
He could not lightly have lingered so long with a lady,
1300. But he had craved a kiss, by his courtesy,
By some touch of some trifle at some tale's end.'
Then quoth Gawain, 'Indeed, let it be as you like;
I shall kiss at your commandment, as befits a knight,
And further, lest he displease you, so plead it no more.'

1305. With that she comes near and catches him in her arms,
      Bends lovingly down and kisses the man.
      They comely commend Christ to each other;
      She goes forth at the door without more ado;
      And (he) prepares to rise and hastens quickly,
1310. Calls for his chamberlain, chooses his weeds,
      Bends his course, when he is ready, blithely to mass;
      And then he went to his meal that duly awaited him,
      And made merry all the day, til the moon rose,
                        with games.
1315.   Never was knight better engaged
                  Between two so worthy dames,
                  The elder and the young;
                  Much pleasure they had together.

VIII

      And always the lord of the land is absorbed in his sports,
1320. To hunt in the holt and heath for barren hinds;
      Such a sum he there slew by the time that the sun set,
      Of does and other deer, to surmise were a wonder.
      Then fiercely they flocked as one folk at the end,
      And quickly of the killed deer a quarry they made.
1325. The best bent thereto with enough men,
      Gathered the greatest in fat that were there,
      And did them dearly dismember as the deed requires;
      Some that were there searched them at the assay,
      Two fingers of fat they found in the leanest of all.
1330. Then they slit the slot, seized the gullet,
      Shaved with a sharp knife, and knit up the flesh;
      Then they ripped the four limbs, and rent off the hide,
      Then they broke open the belly, took out the bowels
      Carefully lest they loosen the ligature of the knot;
1335. They gripped the gorge, and readily removed
      The weasand from the windpipe, and tossed out the guts;

Then they sheared out the shoulders with their sharp knives,
Haled them out by a little hole to have whole sides.
Then they broke open the breast and split it in two,
1340. And again at the gorge begins one then,
Rives it up readily right to the fork,
Voids out the fore-parts, and verily thereafter
All the membranes by the ribs readily they lance;
So by reason they cleared away by the backbone
1345. Even down to the haunch, that hung all together,
And heaved it up all whole, and hewed it off there,
And that they call by the name of numbles, as I believe,
in kind;
By the fork of all the thighs
1350. The flaps they lance behind;
To hew it in two they hie,
By the backbone to unbind.

IX

Both the head and the neck they hewed off then,
And then sunder they the sides swiftly from the chine,
1355. And the raven's fee they threw in a thicket;
Then thirled they either thick side through the ribs,
And hung then either by the hocks of the legs,
Each man for his fee, as befits him to have.
Upon a fell of the fair beast they fed their hounds
1360. With the liver and the lights, the leather of the paunches,
And bread bathed in blood blended thereamong.
Boldly they blew prise, bayed their hounds,
Then they took their flesh, turned toward home,
Sounding full stoutly many stiff notes.
1365. By the time daylight was done the company was all come
Into the comely castle, where the knight bides
full still,
With bliss and bright fire kindled.
The lord is come thereto;

1370.   When Gawain with him met
     There was but weal at will.

X

Then commanded the lord in that hall to summon all the many,
Both the ladies to come below with their maidens
Before all the folk on the floor, the men he bids
1375. Verily his venison to fetch before him,
And all in good sport Gawain he called,
Teaches him the tally of full taut beasts,
Shows him the sheer fat shorn from the ribs.
'How pleases you this play? Have I won praise?
1380. Have I thriving thanks deserved through my craft?'
'Yes, indeed,' quoth that other wight, 'here is the fairest catch
That I have seen this seven years in winter season.'
'And all I give you, Gawain,' quoth the man then,
'For by accord of covenant ye may claim it as your own.'
1385. 'This is sooth,' quoth the man, 'I say the same to you:
What I have worthily won within this dwelling,
Indeed with as good a will is worthy to be yours.'
He hasps his fair neck within his arms,
And kisses him as comely he could devise:
1390. 'Take you there my winnings, I achieved no more;
I vouchsafe it freely, even if it were more.'
'It is good,' quoth the good man, 'many thanks therefor.
It may be such it is the better, if you would brief me on
Where you won this same wealth by your own wit.'
1395. 'That was not the agreement,' quoth he, 'ask me no more.
For you have taken what betides you, expect
          nothing more.'
     They laughed and made merry
     With words that were praiseworthy;
1400.   To supper they went at once,
     With dainties new enough.

XI

Afterwards by the chimney in the chamber they sat,
Wights the fine wine brought to them oft,
And again in their jests they agreed on the morn
1405. To fulfill the same terms they had made before:
Whatever chance so betides their winnings to exchange,
Whatsoever new to take, at night when they met.
They were in accord with the covenant before all the court;
The beverage was brought forth in jest at that time,
1410. Then they graciously took their leave at last,
Each man hastened quickly to his bed.
By the time that the cock had crowed and cackled but thrice
The lord had leaped from his bed, and each one of his men;
So that the meat and the mass was meetly delivered,
1415. The company directed to the wood ere any daybreak,
                to the chase;
        Loud with hunt and horns
        Through plains they pass along,
        Uncoupled among the thorns
1420.   Hounds that ran headlong.

XII

Soon they call for a quest on the marsh side,
The huntsman urged the hounds that first picked up the scent,
Wild words he uttered with a loud noise;
The hounds that heard it hastened thither swiftly,
1425. And turned as fast to the trail, forty at once;
Then such a hue and cry of gathered hounds
Arose that the rocks rang about;
Hunters spurred them on with horn and mouth.
Then all in a throng they rushed off together
1430. Between a pool in that wood and a rugged crag;
On a knoll by a cliff, at the marsh side,
Where the rough rocks unruly had fallen,

They fared to the find, and the men after them;
They encircled the crag and the knoll both,
1435. Wights, while they well wist that it were within,
The beast that was noted there by the bloodhounds.
Then they beat among the bushes, and bid him uprise,
And he unsoundly sought out athwart the men;
One of the most wondrous swine dashed out there,
1440. Long since estranged from the herd due to age,
For he was burly and broad, the greatest of all boars,
Full grim when he grunted; then many grieved,
For three at the first thrust he threw to the earth,
And spurred forth good speed without more ado.
1445. The others hollered hi! full high, and hey! hey! cried,
Had horns to mouth, eagerly recheated;
Many were the merry sounds of men and hounds
That hurried after this boar with boast and with outcry
                    to kill.
1450.   Full oft he bides at bay,
             And maims the pack in melee;
             He hurts some of the hounds, and they
             Full piteously yowl and yell.

XIII

Men to shoot at him show themselves then,
1455. Harry him with their arrows, hit him often;
But the points were impaired by the pith in his shoulders,
Though the shaven shaft shattered in pieces,
And the barbs would not bite on his brow;
The head hopped again wheresoever it hit.
1460. But when the dints of the doughty strokes harmed him,
Then, brain-mad for strife, on the men he rushes,
Hurts them full fiercely where he hurries forth,
And many were terrified thereat, and withdrew a little.
But the lord on a light horse launches after him,
1465. Like a man bold for the battlefield his bugle he blows,

He recheated, and rode through undergrowth full thick,
Pursuing this wild swine til the sun set.
This day with this same doing they drive in this wise,
While our lovely man lies in his bed,
1470. Gawain happily at home, in garments full rich
      of hue.
    The lady did not forget
    To come to greet him;
    Full early she was at him
1475.   His mood for to remove.

XIV

She comes to the curtain, and peeps at the knight.
Sir Gawain welcomed her worthily at once,
And she full eagerly yields him her words in return,
Sits herself softly by his side, and swiftly she laughs,
1480. And with a lovely look she laid on him these words:
'Sir, if ye be Gawain, a wonder methink it,
A wight that is so well inclined always to good,
And cannot understand the manners of society;
And if one teaches you them, you cast them from your mind;
1485. Thou hast forgotten promptly what I taught ye yesterday
By the elder-truest token of talk that I could.'
'What is that?' quoth the wight, 'Indeed I know not;
If it be sooth that ye say, the blame is mine own.'
'Yet I acquainted you with kissing,' quoth the fair lady then,
1490. 'Quickly to claim wherever countenance is couth;
That becomes such a knight that practices courtesy.'
'Do away,' quoth that doughty man, 'my dear lady, with that speech;
For that I durst not do, lest I were refused.
If I were denied, I were wrong indeed if I offered.'
1495. 'My faith,' quoth the merry wife, 'ye may not be denied,
Ye are stalwart enough to constrain with strength, if you like,
If any were so villainous as to refuse you.'
'Yes, by God,' quoth Gawain, 'good is your speech;

But threat is ignoble in the land where I come from,
1500.   And each gift that is not given with good will.
I am at your command, to kiss when you like,
Ye may seize when you wish, and cease when you think,
          in time.'
      The lady bends down
1505.   And sweetly kisses his face;
      Much speech they there expound
      Of love-making's grief and grace.

XV

'I want to know from you, wight,' that worthy one then said,
'If you be not wroth therewith, what the reason is
1510.   That so young and so bold as ye at this time,
So courteous, so knightly, as ye are known out there —
And of all chivalry to choose, the chief thing praised
Is the loyal sport of love, the science of arms;
For to tell of this striving of these true knights,
1515.   It is the written token and text of their works;
How knights for their true love have ventured their lives,
Endured for their sweetheart doleful hours,
And after avenged with their valor and voided their care,
And brought bliss into the bower with bounties their own —
1520.   And ye are the comeliest natured knight of your era,
Your fame and your renown are known everywhere,
And I have sat by you here two separate times,
Yet never heard I no words your head held
That ever referred to love, no less no more;
1525.   And ye, that are so courteous and gracious in your vows,
Ought to be eager to show a young thing
And teach some tokens of true love crafts.
What, are ye ill-bred, that all this fame wields?
Or else ye deem me too dull to hearken to your dalliance?
1530.   For shame!

I come hither single, and sit
To learn from you some game;
Do so, teach me of your wit
While my lord is from home.'

XVI

1535. 'In good faith,' quoth Gawain, 'may God repay you!'
Great is the good glee, and a huge game to me,
That one so worthy as ye would wend hither,
And pain yourself with so poor a man, as to play with your knight
With any kind of favor, it gives me pleasure;
1540. But to take the trouble upon myself to expound true love,
And touch upon the themes of text and tales of arms
To you that, I know well, wield more skill
In that art, by half, or a hundred of such
As I am, or ever shall, while I live on earth,
1545. It were a folly manifold, my lady, by my troth.
I would your willing worker be at my might,
As I am highly beholden, and evermore will
Be servant to yourself, may the Lord save me!'
Thus that lady questioned him, and tested him oft,
1550. For to have won him to woe, whatever else she thought;
But he defended himself so fair that no fault appeared,
Nor no evil on either side, nothing they knew
            but bliss.
      They laughed and sported long;
1555.   At last she did him kiss,
      Her leave fair she took,
      And went her way indeed.

XVII

Then the man rouses himself and rises for mass,
And after that their dinner was prepared and clearly served.

1560. The knight sported with the ladies all day,
   But the lord launched over the land full oft,
   Pursues his mischievous swine, that swings by the banks
   And bit the best of his hounds their backs asunder
   Where he bode at bay, til bowmen broke it,
1565. And made him despite his will move into the open,
   So fell flew arrows there when the folk gathered.
   But yet the stoutest he made to start at times
   Til at last he was so weary he might run no more,
   But in what haste he might he wins his way to a hole
1570. To a ledge by a rock where runs the stream.
   He gets the bank at his back, begins to scrape,
   The froth foamed at the corners of his ugly mouth,
   Whets his white tusks; irked with him then were
   All the men so bold that stood by him
1575. To nick him from afar, but none durst approach him
        for danger;
      He had hurt so many before,
      That all were then full loath
      To be more with his tusks torn,
1580.   That was fierce and brain-mad both.

XVIII

Then the knight came himself, spurring his horse,
   Saw him abide at bay, his men beside;
   He alights lovingly, leaves his courser,
   Draws out a bright blade and strides forth mightily,
1585. Fares fast through the ford where the fierce one abides.
   The wild beast was aware of the wight with weapon in hand,
   His hair highly heaved, so violently he snorted
   That many feared for the man, lest the worst befall him.
   The swine sets straight out at the man,
1590. So that the man and the boar were both in a heap
   In the whitest of the water: that other had it the worse,
   For the man marked him well when they first met,

Solidly set the blade even in the breast,
Hit him up to the hilt, so that the heart was sundered,

1595.   And snarling he yielded, and went downstream
full tilt.
A hundred hounds seized him,
That fiercely did him bite,
Men brought him to open field,

1600.   And dogs dictated death to him.

XIX

There was blowing of prise in many a loud horn,
Great shouting on high by men that might;
Hounds bayed at that beast, as bidden by their masters
That were the chief hunters of that burdensome chase.

1605.   Then a wight that was wise in woodcraft
Begins to cut up this boar beautifully.
First he hews off his head and sets it on high,
And then rends him roughly all along the spine,
Pulls out the entrails, grills them on a fire,

1610.   With bread blended therewith rewards his hounds.
Then he breaks out the brawn in bright broad chunks,
Has the haslets out, as is highly fitting;
And yet he fastens all whole the halves together,
And then on a stiff stake hangs him proudly.

1615.   Now with this same swine they swing home;
The boar's head was borne before the man himself
That had felled him in the ford through force of his hand
so strong.
Til he saw Sir Gawain

1620.   In the hall the wait seemed full long;
He called, and Gawain gamely came
His fees therefor to claim.

XX

The lord full loud with speech and laughter merry,
When he saw Sir Gawain, with delight he speaks;
1625. The good ladies were gotten, and the many gathered,
He shows them the shoulders, and shapes for them the tale
Of the boar's largeness and length, the wickedness also
Of the war with the wild swine in the wood where he fled.
That other knight full comely commended his deeds,
1630. And praised it as a great prize that he had achieved,
For such a brawn of a beast, the bold man said,
Nor such sides of a swine he never saw before.
Then they handled the huge head, the polite man praised it,
And acted repulsed thereat to honor the lord.
1635. 'Now, Gawain,' quoth the good man, 'this game is your own
By agreement final and fast, as in faith ye know.'
'It is sooth,' quoth the man, 'and surely as true
All I get I shall give again, by my troth.'
He clasped the knight about the neck, and courteously kisses him,
1640. And again of the same he served him there.
'Now we are even,' quoth the noble one, 'in this eventide,
Of all the covenants that we knit, since I came hither,
                    by law.'
            The lord said, 'By Saint Giles,
1645.   Ye are the best that I know!
                Ye shall be rich in a while,
                If ye keep trading so.'

XXI

Then they set tables aloft on trestles,
Cast cloths upon them; clear light then
1650. Wakened on walls from waxen torches;
Men were seated and served all about in the hall;
Much mirth and glee sprang up therein
About the fire on the floor, and in various ways

At the supper and after, many noble songs,
1655. Such as Christmas tunes and carols new,
With all the mannerly mirth that man may tell of.
And ever our lovely knight beside the lady,
Such a seemly semblance to that man she made,
With silent stolen countenance, that stalwart to please,
1660. That all astonished was the wight, and wroth with himself,
But he would not for his breeding speak against her,
But dealt with her all in daintiness, howsoever the deed be
distorted.
When they had played in the hall
1665. As long as their desire lasted,
To the chamber the lord called him,
And to the chimney they passed.

XXII

And there they drank, had dealings, and deemed once more
To continue on the same note on New Year's Eve;
1670. But the knight craved leave to proceed on the morn,
For it was near the term that he had to keep.
The lord hindered him in that, begged him to remain,
And said, 'As I am an honest man, I give my word
Thou shall achieve the green chapel thy chore to perform,
1675. Sir, at New Year's light, long before prime.
Therefore lie thou in thy loft and take thine ease,
And I shall hunt in this wood, and hold to the terms,
Exchange the winnings when I return hither;
For I have tested thee twice, and faithful I find thee.
1680. Now 'third time throw best' remember on the morn,
Make we merry while we may and be mindful of joy,
For misery may seize whenever we please.'
This was readily granted, and Gawain remained,
Drink was blithely brought him, and they went to bed
1685. with light.
Sir Gawain lies and sleeps

Full still and soft all night;
The lord that his crafts keeps,
Full early he was dressed.

XXIII

1690. After mass a morsel he and his men took;
Merry was the morning, his mount he requests.
All the men on horse that should come after him
Were promptly prepared on their steed before the hall gates.
Wondrously fair was the field, for the frost clung;
1695. In red riddled upon the rack rises the sun,
And full clear casts off the clouds of the welkin.
Hunters unleashed hounds by the edge of a wood,
Rocks rang by a copse with the noise of their horns;
Some fell on the scent where the fox bode,
1700. Trails traversing often in the trickery of their wiles;
A small hound cries thereof, a huntsman calls to him;
His fellows fall in with him, panting full thick,
Run forth in a rabble right on the track,
And he scampers before them; they found him soon,
1705. And when they saw him with their eyes they pursued him fast,
Assailing him full plainly with a wrathful noise;
And he twists and turns through many a dense grove,
Doubles back, and hearkens by hedges full oft.
At last by a little ditch he leaps over a hedge,
1710. Steals out full silently by the edge of a marsh,
Believed to have of the woods with his wiles escaped the hounds;
Then was he come, ere he wist, to an excellent hunting station,
There three fierce ones in throng threaten him at once,
          all gray.
1715.   He turned again quickly,
        And stiffly started astray,
        With all the woe on earth
        To the wood he went away.

XXIV

Then it was a delight in life to listen to the hounds,
1720. When all the pack had met him, mingled together:
Such a curse at that sight they set on his head
As if all the clambering cliffs had clattered in a heap;
Here he was hallooed, when the men met him,
Loudly he was greeted with snarling speech;
1725. There he was threatened and often thief called,
And always the tattlers at his tail, that he might not tarry.
Often he was run at, when he ran off,
And often reeled in again, so wily was Reynard.
And yea, he led them as laggards, the lord and his company,
1730. In this manner by the mountains until midday,
While the noble knight at home wholesomely sleeps
Within the comely curtains, on the cold morn.
But the lady for love let herself not sleep,
Nor the purpose to impair that was pitched in her heart,
1735. But rose up promptly, rushed thither
In a merry mantle, reaching to the ground,
That was furled full fine with pelt well-trimmed;
No good covering on her head but the finer stones
Traced about her head-dress in clusters of twenty;
1740. Her worthy face and her throat displayed all naked,
Her breast bare before, and behind as well.
She comes within the chamber door, and closes it after her,
Throws open a window, and on the wight calls,
And quickly thus chided him with her rich words,
1745.   with cheer:
        'Ah, man, how can you sleep,
        This morning is so clear?'
        He was in drowsing deep,
        But then he could her hear.

XXV

1750. In dreary drooping of dream driveled that noble,
　　　　Like a man that was in mourning about many persistent thoughts,
　　　　How destiny should that day deal him his fate
　　　　At the green chapel, when he meets the man,
　　　　And behooves his buffet abide without more debate;
1755. But when that comely one came he recovered his wits,
　　　　Swings out of his dreams, and answers with haste.
　　　　The lady lovely came laughing sweetly,
　　　　Fell over his fair face, and fetchingly kissed him;
　　　　He welcomes her worthily with noble cheer.
1760. He sees her so glorious and gaily attired,
　　　　So faultless in her features and of such fine hues,
　　　　Strong welling joy warmed his heart.
　　　　With smiling smooth and pleasant they plunged into mirth,
　　　　That all that passed between them was bliss and good fortune
1765. 　　　　　　　　　and joy.
　　　　　　　　They lanced words good,
　　　　　　　　Much weal then was therein;
　　　　　　　　Great peril between them stood,
　　　　　　　　If Mary did not mind her knight.

XXVI

1770. For that princess of preeminence pressed him so thick,
　　　　Urged him so near the edge that he must needs
　　　　Either receive there her love or loathly refuse.
　　　　He cared for his courtesy, lest he were craven,
　　　　And more for his mischief if he should sin,
1775. And be traitor to that man that owned that dwelling.
　　　　'God shield me,' quoth he, 'that shall not befall!'
　　　　With a little loving laugh he laid aside
　　　　All the speeches of special affection that sprang from her mouth.
　　　　Quoth that woman to the man, 'Blame ye deserve
1780. If ye love not that life that ye lie next to,

Wounded in heart more than all the wights in the world,
But if ye have a mistress, a lover, that you like better,
And have plighted faith to that noble one, fastened so hard
That you list not lose it — and that I believe now;
1785. And I truly pray you that ye tell me that now,
For all the loves in life do not hide the truth
             with guile.'
        The knight said, 'By Saint John,'
        And smoothly did he smile,
1790.   'In faith, I have right none,
        Nor will want one the while.'

XXVII

'That is a word,' quoth that woman, 'that worst is of all,
But I am answered forsooth, sorry that seems to me.
Kiss me now comely, and I shall take myself hence,
1795. I may but mourn upon earth, as a maid that loves much.'
Sighing she swayed down and seemly him kissed,
And then she severs from him, and says as she stands,
'Now, dear, at this departing do me this favor,
Give me something as a gift, your glove if it were,
1800. That I be reminded of thee, man, my mourning to lessen!'
'Now indeed,' quoth that wight, 'I would I had here
The dearest thing I own in the world for thy love,
For ye have deserved, forsooth, wondrously oft
More reward by right than I might render;
1805. But to give you as a love-token what amounted to little,
It is not to your honor to have at this time
A glove for a garrison of Gawain's gifts;
And I am here on an errand in lands unknown,
And have no men with bags full of gracious things;
1810. That mislikes me, lady, for your sake,
Each man must do as he must, take it not amiss nor
             in pain.'
        'Nay, sir of high honors,'

1815.
> Quoth that lovely one in linen,
> 'Though I had nought of yours,
> Yet should ye have of mine.'

XXVIII

She offered him a rich ring of red-gold work,
With a sparkling stone standing aloft
That bore blinking beams as the bright sun —
1820. Wit ye well, it was worth wealth full huge.
But the man refused it, and readily he said,
'I want no gifts, before God, my gay one, at this time;
I have none to offer you, nor nought will I take.'
She bade it him full busily, and he her bode denies,
1825. And swears swiftly by his sooth that he would not seize it,
And she sorrowed that he forsook it, and said thereafter,
'If ye reject my ring, for it seems too rich,
And ye would not be so highly beholden to me,
I shall give you my girdle, that gains you less.'
1830. She undid a belt lightly that linked around her sides.
Knit upon her kirtle under the bright mantle;
Adorned it was with green silk and with gold trimmed,
Nought but braided around, done by hand;
And this she offered to the man, and blithely besought,
1835. Though it unworthy were, that he would take it.
And he denied that he would never accept in no wise
Neither gold nor garrison ere God sent him the grace
To achieve the exploit he had chosen there.
'And therefore, I pray you, be not displeased,
1840. And cease your business, for I shall never consent to grant
> it you.
> I am dearly to you beholden
> Because of your demeanor,
> And ever in hot and cold
1845.
> Shall be your true servant.'

XXIX

'Now, do you forsake this silk,' said the woman then,
'For it is simple in itself? and so well it seems.
Lo, so little is it, and less is it worth;
But whoever knew the qualities that knit are therein,
1850. He would appraise it at a higher price, peradventure.
For whatever man is girt with this green lace,
While he has it fittingly fastened about,
There is no man under heaven who can hew him,
For he cannot be slain by any sleight upon earth.'
1855. Then pondered the knight, and it came into his heart
That it were a jewel for the jeopardy adjudged to him:
When he reached the chapel to meet his destiny,
If he might have slipped out unslain, the sleight were noble.
Then he put up with her persistence and permitted her to speak,
1860. And she pressed on him the belt and offered it him forthwith —
And he granted it and gave in with a good will —
And she besought him, for her sake, to reveal it never,
But to loyally conceal it from her lord; the man consents
That no wight should ever know of it, indeed, but they two
1865.   alone.
           He thanked her oft full earnestly,
           Full through with heart and thought.
           By then three times
           She has kissed the knight so taut.

XXX

1870. Then she takes her leave, and leaves him there,
For more mirth of that man might she not get.
When she was gone, Sir Gawain gears himself soon,
Rises and enriches himself in noble array,
Lays up the love-lace the lady gave him,
1875. Hid it full graciously, where he could find it again.
Then chiefly to the chapel he chooses the way,

Privily approached a priest, and prayed him there
That he would hear his confession and teach him better
How his soul should be saved when he should go hence.
1880. There he shrove himself sheerly and showed his misdeeds,
Of the major and the minor, and mercy beseeches,
And of absolution he on the man calls;
And he absolved him surely and set him so clean
As if doomsday were arranged on the morn.
1885. And then he makes merry among the noble ladies,
With comely carols and all kinds of joy,
As never he did but that day, til the dark night,
      with bliss.
    Each man had delight there
1890.   From him, and said, 'Indeed,
    Thus merry was he never
    Since he came hither, ere this!'

XXXI

Now may he linger in that lee, there may love betide him!
Yet is the lord on the land, leading his game.
1895. He has headed off this fox that he followed long;
As he sprang over a hedge to spy the shrew,
There as he heard the hounds that pressed him hard,
Reynard came running through a rough grove
And all the rabble in a rush right at his heels.
1900. The wight was aware of the wild one, and warily abides,
And draws out the bright blade, and casts at the beast.
And he shrank from the sharp blade, and would have reared back;
A hound hastens to him, right ere he might,
And right before the horse's feet they all fell on him,
1905. And worried now this wily one with a wrathful noise.
The lord alights quickly, and snatches him at once,
Raised him full readily out of the hounds' mouths,
Holds him high over his head, hallooes loudly,
And there bayed about him many fierce hounds.

1910. Huntsmen hied him thither with horns full many,
Always sounding the recheat aright til they saw the man.
By the time that noble company was come
All that ever bore bugle blew at once,
And all those others hallooed that had no horns;
1915. It was the merriest cry of hounds that ever men heard,
The rich uproar that was raised there for Reynard's soul
with din.
Their hounds they there reward,
Their heads they fondle and caress,
1920. And then they took Reynard
And stripped off his coat.

XXXII

And then they held for home, for it was nigh night,
Sounding full stoutly in their fierce horns.
The lord is alighted at last at his dear home,
1925. Finds fire in the hall, the knight there beside,
Sir Gawain the good, that glad was withal,
He led much joy among the ladies for love.
He wore a tunic of blue that extended to the earth,
His softly furred surcoat suited him well,
1930. And his hood of the same hung on his shoulder,
Blended all of white fur were both all about.
He meets this good man in the middle of the floor,
And all with delight he greets him, and goodly he said,
'I shall fulfill first our agreement now,
1935. That we had speedily spoken when there was spared no drink.'
Then embraces he the knight and kisses him thrice,
As savorly and seriously as he could set on him.
'By Christ,' quoth that other knight, 'ye catch much happiness
In exchange of this merchandise, if ye had good bargains.'
1940. 'Yes, price is no problem,' quoth chiefly that other,
'So long as promptly paid is the purchase that I owe for,'
'Mary,' quoth that other man, 'mine is behind,

For I have hunted all this day, and nought have I got
But this foul fox fell — the fiend take the goods!
1945. And that is full poor to pay for such prized things
As ye have boldly thrust on me here, such three kisses
so good.'
'Enough,' quoth Sir Gawain,
I thank you, by the rood';
1950. And how the fox was slain
He told him as they stood.

XXXIII

With mirth and minstrelsy, with meat at their will,
They made as merry as men might
With laughing of ladies, with words of jest.
1955. Gawain and the good man, so glad were they both
As if the company were crazed, or else been drunk.
Both the lord and his household made many jokes
Til the season was seen that they must sever;
At last it behooved them to go to their beds.
1960. Then humbly his leave by the lord first
This noble man takes, and fair he him thanks:
'For such a marvelous sojourn as I have had here,
For your honor at this high feast, may the high King repay you!
I offer myself as one of yours, if you like,
1965. For I must needs, as ye know, move on tomorrow,
And if ye entrust some man to teach me, as ye promised,
The path to the green chapel, as God will suffer me
To deal on New Year's Day with the doom of my destiny.'
'In good faith,' quoth the good man, 'with a good will
1970. All that I ever promised you shall I readily hold to.'
There assigns he a servant to set him on the way,
And conduct him by the downs, so that he had no delay,
For to push through the field and fare quickest
by the grove.
1975. The lord Gawain did thank,

Such worship he would him weave.
Then from those ladies noble
The knight has taken his leave.

XXXIV

With care and with kissing he addresses them both,
1980. And many profuse thanks he pressed them to accept,
And they right away returned him the same.
They commended him to Christ with full cold sighs.
Then from the household he reverently departs;
Each man that he met, he gave him thanks,
1985. For his service and his solace and his special pains,
That they with busyness had been about him to serve;
And each man as sorry to sever with him there
As if they had dwelled worthily with that gentleman ever.
Then with servants and light he was led to his chamber,
1990. And blithely brought to his bed to be at his rest.
Whether or not he slept soundly I dare not say,
For he had much on the morn to mind, if he would,
            in thought.
        Let him lie there still,
1995.   He nearly has what he sought;
        And if ye will be still a while,
        I shall tell you how things wrought.

FITT 4

I

Now nears the New Year, and the night passes,
The day drives away the dark, as the Lord bids;
2000. But wild weathers of the world wakened out there,
Clouds cast keenly the cold to the earth,
With near enough of the north the naked to distress.
The snow fell full sharply, that snipped at the wild creatures;
The warbling wind gusted from the heights,
2005. And drove each dale full of drifts full great.
The man listened full well that lay in his bed,
Though he locks his lids, full little he sleeps;
By each cock that crew he knew well the appointed time.
Deftly he got dressed, ere the day dawned,
2010. For there was light of a lamp that gleamed in his chamber;
He called to his chamberlain, who promptly answered him,
And bade him bring him his byrnie and saddle his horse;
That other starts up and fetches him his weeds,
And arrays Sir Gawain in a great wise.
2015. First he clad him in his clothes to ward off the cold,

And then his other armor, that was kindly kept,
Both his pauncer and his plate, polished full clean,
The rings of his rich byrnie rocked free of the rust;
And all was fresh as at first, and he was fain then
2020.   to give thanks.
            He had on each piece,
            Wiped full well and nobly;
            The gayest knight from here to Greece
            Bid the man bring his horse.

II

2025. While the noblest weeds he throws on himself —
      His coat with the emblem of the clear symbols
      Environed upon velvet, virtuous stones
      Embossed and bounded about, embroidered seams,
      And fair-furred within with fair skins —
2030. Yet he left not the lace, the lady's gift,
      That Gawain did not forget for his own good.
      When he had belted his blade upon his bulging haunches,
      Then dressed he his love-token about him double,
      Swiftly swathed around his waist sweetly that knight
2035. The girdle of green silk, that gay well beseemed
      Upon that royal red cloth that showed so rich.
      But wore not this same wight for wealth this girdle,
      For pride of the pendants, though polished they were,
      And though the glittering gold glistened upon the ends,
2040. But for to save himself, when it behove him to suffer,
      To abide bane without debate of blade to defend him
                              or knife.
            When the bold man was dressed
            He went out in a trice,
2045.   All the renowned household
            He thanks oft full rife.

III

Then was Gringolet made ready, that was great and huge,
And had been stabled savorly in a secure wise,
He wishes to gallop for conditioning, that proud horse then.
2050. The wight goes up to him and looks at his coat,
And said soberly to himself and by his sooth swears:
'Here is a company in this castle that keeps courtesy in mind,
The master maintains them, joy may they have;
This dear lady during her life may love betide her;
2055. If they for charity cherish a guest,
And uphold honor in their hand, may the noble one repay them
That upholds the heaven on high, and also you all!
And if I might life upon earth lead for any while,
I should grant you some reward readily, if I might.'
2060. Then steps he into the stirrups and strides aloft;
His servant showed him his shield, on his shoulder he latched it,
Goads Gringolet with his gilt heels,
And he starts onto the stone, he stood no longer
                         to prance.
2065.   His man on horse was then,
          That bore his spear and lance.
          'This castle to Christ I commend:
          May He give it always good fortune.'

IV

The bridge was lowered, and the broad gates
2070. Unbarred and laid open on both sides.
The man blessed himself quickly, and the planks crossed —
Praises the porter who knelt before the prince,
Gives him God and good day, that Gawain he save —
And went on his way with his one wight,
2075. That should teach him to turn toward that troublesome place
Where the rueful cut he should receive.
They bent their course by banks where boughs are bare,

They climbed by cliffs where clings the cold.
The heaven was upheld, but ugly thereunder;
2080. Mist drizzled on the moor, melted on the mountains,
Each hill had a hat, a mist-mantle huge.
Brooks boiled and broke along the banks,
Sheer splashing of shores where they shoved down.
Well wild was the way by the woods where they must go,
2085. Til it was soon the season when the sun rises
at that time.
They were on a hill full high,
The white snow lay beside;
The man that rode with him
2090. Bade his master abide.

V

'For I have brought you hither, sir, at this time,
And now ye are not far from that noted place
That ye have searched and enquired so specially after;
But I shall say you for sooth, since I know you,
2095. And ye are a man alive that I well love,
If ye would heed my advice, it would be better for ye.
The place that ye press to full perilous is held;
There dwells a wight in that waste, the worst upon earth,
For he is stiff and stern, and loves to strike,
2100. And more he is than any man upon middle-earth,
And his body bigger than the four best
That are in Arthur's house, Hector, or any other.
He gets his chance at the green chapel,
Where none passes by that place so proud in his arms
2105. That he does not beat him to death by dint of his hand;
For he is a ruthless man, and never shows mercy,
For be it churl or chaplain that by the chapel rides,
Monk or mass-priest, or any man else,
He thinks it as pleasing to kill him as to go on living himself.
2110. Therefore I say to thee, as sooth as ye in saddle sit,

Come ye there, ye will be killed, if I may advise the knight;
Ye may trust me truly, though ye had twenty lives
               to spend.
        He has dwelt here full yore,
2115.   On the battlefield much strife bent,
        Against his dints sore
        Ye may not yourself defend.

VI

'Therefore, good Sir Gawain, let the man alone,
And get away through some other gate, for God's sake!
2120. Proceed by some other region, there Christ may you speed,
And I shall hie me home again, and promise you further
That I shall swear by God and all his good saints,
So help me God and the halidom, and oaths enough,
That I shall loyally keep your secret, and never utter a word
2125. That ever ye sought to flee from a man that I knew.'
'Gramercy,' quoth Gawain, and grudgingly he said,
'Well I wish thee, wight, that would my good,
And to loyally keep my secret I believe well thou would.
But held thou to it never so fast, and I here passed,
2130. Hastened in fear for to flee, in the form that thou tells,
I were a knight coward, I might not be excused.
But I will to the chapel, whatever chance may befall
And talk with that same man the tale that I please,
Whether it be weal or woe, as fate would
2135.   have it.
        Though he be a stern knave
        To set straight, and stands with stave,
        Full well can the Lord shape
        His servants for to save.'

VII

2140. 'Mary!' quoth that other man, 'now thou declares so much
       That thou wilt thine own annoyance take on thyself,
       And if thee list to lose thy life, I will not hinder or keep thee.
       Have here thy helm on thy head, thy spear in thy hand,
       And ride down this same path beside yon rock,
2145. Til thou be brought to the bottom of the wild valley;
       Then look a little in the glade on thy left hand,
       And thou shall see in that dell the very chapel,
       And the burly man of battle that keeps it.
       Now farewell, in God's name, Gawain the noble!
2150. For all the gold on earth I would not go with thee,
       Nor bear thee fellowship through this forest one foot further.'
       With that the wight in the wood wends his bridle,
       Hit the horse with his heels as hard as he might,
       Gallops over the land, and leaves the knight there
2155.   all alone.
                'By God himself,' quoth Gawain,
                'I will neither weep nor groan;
                To God's will I am fully inclined,
                And to him I am committed.'

VIII

2160. Then he spurs Gringolet and picks up the path,
       Shoves in by a shore at the side of a copse,
       Rides through the rough bank right to the dale;
       And then he looked about, and he thought it wild,
       And saw no sign of shelter anywhere,
2165. But huge and steep banks upon both sides,
       And rugged, knuckled crags with gnarled stones;
       It seemed to him that the skies were grazed by the jutting rocks.
       Then he halted, and withheld his horse at that time,
       And oft turned his face to seek the chapel.
2170. He saw no such thing on any side, and strange it seemed

Save, a little way off in a glade, a mound as it were;
A round barrow on a bank beside the water's edge,
By the force of a flood that flowed there;
The spring bubbled therein as though it had boiled.

2175. The knight urges his horse and comes to the mound,
Alights lovingly, and at a linden tree attaches
The reins and his rich steed with a rough branch.
Then he goes to the barrow, about it he walks,
Debating with himself what it might be.

2180. It had a hole on the end and on either side,
And was overgrown with grass in patches everywhere,
And all was hollow within, nothing but an old cave,
Or a crevice of an old crag, he could not say
          for sure.

2185.   'Whee, lord!' quoth the gentle knight,
       'Could this be the green chapel?
       Here might about midnight
       The devil his matins tell!'

IX

'Now indeed,' quoth Gawain, 'it is deserted here;

2190. The oratory is ugly, with herbs overgrown;
Well beseems the wight clad in green
To deal here his devotion in the devil's wise.
Now I feel it is the fiend, in my five wits,
That has stuck me with the summons to destroy me here.

2195. This is a chapel of mischance, may evil befall it!
It is the cursedest church that I ever came in!'
With high helm on his head, his lance in his hand,
He roams up to the roof of that rough dwelling.
Then heard he from that high hill, in a hard rock

2200. Beyond the brook, on a bank, a wondrous loud noise:
What! It clattered in the cliff, as if it should cleave,
As if one upon a grindstone had ground a scythe.
What! It whirred and whetted, as water at a mill;

What! It rushed and rang, ruth to hear.
2205. Then 'By God,' quoth Gawain, 'that apparatus, as I believe,
Is arranged out of reverence for me, a man of rank, to be met
en route.
God's will be done! "Alas"
It helps me not a jot.
2210.   My life though I forgo,
No noise do I dread.'

X

Then the knight called out full loud,
'Who rules in this stead to hold a tryst with me?
For now is good Gawain going right here.
2215. If any wight wants aught, come hither fast
Either now or never, his needs to speed.'
'Abide,' quoth one on the bank above his head,
'And thou shall have all in haste that I once promised thee.'
Yet he rushed on with that clamor rashly for a while,
2220. And with whetting turned away, ere he would alight;
And then he passes by a crag, and comes out of a hole,
Whirling out of a corner with a fierce weapon,
A Danish axe newly done, the dint to deliver,
With a burly blade bent back upon the shaft,
2225. Sharpened on a whetstone, four foot large —
It was no less, by the lace that gleamed full bright —
And the man in the green attired as at first,
Both the face and the legs, locks and beard,
Save that he hastened with his feet fairly on the ground,
2230. Set the steel to the stone and stalked beside.
When he went to the water, there he would not wade,
He hopped over his axe, and valiantly strides,
Very fierce on a field that was broad about,
                on snow.
2235.   Sir Gawain met the knight,
He did not bow to him at all low;

The other said, 'Now, sweet sir,
In trysts a man may thee trust.'

XI

'Gawain,' quoth that green man, 'May God keep you!
2240. Indeed thou art welcome, wight, to my place,
And thou hast timed thy travel as a true man should,
And thou knowest the covenant made between us:
At this time twelve month ago thou took what fell to thee,
And I should at this New Year promptly thee requite.
2245. And we are in this valley verily on our own;
Here are no men to part us, reel us as we like.
Take thy helm off thy head, and have here thy pay.
Make no more resistance than I offered thee then
When thou whipped off my head with a single whop.'
2250. 'Nay, by God,' quoth Gawain, 'that gave me a soul,
I shall grudge thee not a whit for any grief that occurs.
But limit thee to one stroke, and I shall stand still
And issue thee no warning to not do as thee like,
nowhere.'
2255. He leaned with his neck, and bowed,
And showed that flesh all bare,
And let on as though he feared nought;
For dread he would not cower.

XII

Then the man in green quickly got ready,
2260. Gathers up his grim tool Gawain to smite;
With all the strength in his body he bore it aloft,
Swung as mightily as mar him he would;
Had he driven down as heavily as he intended,
Who was doughty ever would have been dead there from this dint.
2265. But Gawain glanced sideways at that battle-axe,

As it came gliding down on earth to destroy him,
And shrank a little with the shoulders from the sharp iron.
That other man with a shunt the shiny blade withheld,
And then reproved he the prince with many proud words:
2270. 'Thou art not Gawain,' quoth the man, 'that is held as so good,
That never quailed for no army by hill or by vale,
And now thou flees for fear ere thou feel harm!
Such cowardice of that knight could I never hear.
Neither flinched I nor flew, man, when thou took aim,
2275. Nor cast no cavillation in King Arthur's house.
My head flew to my feet, and yet I never fled;
And thou, ere any harm received, are timid at heart.
Wherefore the better man I ought to be called
therefore.'
2280.   Quoth Gawain, 'I shunt once,
      And so I will no more;
      But should my head fall on the stones,
      I cannot it restore.

XIII

'But haste, man, by thy faith, and bring me to the point.
2285. Deal to me my destiny, and do it out of hand,
For I shall stand thee a stroke, and start no more
Til thy axe has hit me: have here my troth.'
'Have at thee then!' quoth that other, and heaves it aloft,
And looked as angry as though he were mad.
2290. He aims mightily at him, but touches not the man,
Withheld suddenly his hand ere it might injure.
Gawain abides it readily, and not a limb flinches,
But stood still as a stone or else a stump
That intertwined is in rocky ground with hundreds of roots.
2295. Then merrily again did he speak, the man in green,
'So, now that thou has thy heart whole, it behooves me to hit.
Uphold thee now thy high hood that Arthur gave thee,
And save thy neck from this stroke, if it may protect you.'

Gawain full fiercely with wrath then said:
2300. 'Why! Thrash on, thou angry man, thou threatens too long;
     I suspect thy heart takes fright with thine own self.'
     'Forsooth,' quoth that other man, 'so fiercely thou speaks,
     I will no longer in delay leave your errand
                right now.'
2305.   Then takes he his stance to strike,
              And frowns both lip and brow,
              No wonder if he mislike
              That has no hope of rescue.

XIV

     He lifts lightly his weapon, and lets it down fair
2310. With the barb of the blade by the bare neck;
     Though he hammered keenly, hurt him none the more
     But grazed him on that one side, that severed the hide.
     The sharp blade shrank into the flesh through the sheer fat,
     So that the shiny blood over his shoulders shot to the earth;
2315. And when the man saw the blood gleam on the snow,
     He leaped forward with both feet more than a spear length,
     Seized roughly his helm, and threw it on his head
     Jerked with his shoulders to get his fair shield around,
     Draws out a bright sword, and fiercely he speaks —
2320. Never since he was a man born of his mother
     Was he ever in this world a wight half so blithe —
     'Cease, man, from thy violence, offer me no more!
     I have a stroke in this stead without strife taken,
     And if thou direct any more, I readily shall requite,
2325. And quickly return again — and thereto ye may trust —
             And as a foe.
              But one stroke here to me falls —
              The covenant was shaped so,
              Formed in Arthur's halls —
2330.   And therefore, sir, now whoa!'

XV

The knight held off, and on his axe rested,
Set the shaft upon the ground and leaned on the sharp blade,
And looked at the man that went on the land,
How that doughty one, dauntless, daringly stands there
2335. Armed, full fearless: his heart is pleased.
Then he spoke merrily with a loud voice,
And in a ringing tone he said to the man:
'Bold warrior, on this field be not so angry.
No man here has ill-used thee unmannerly,
2340. Nor did but as the covenant at king's court decreed.
I promised thee a stroke and thou hast it; think thee well-paid;
I release thee from the remnant of all other rights.
If I had been agile, a buffet perhaps
More wrathful I could have laid out, to have wrought thee to anger.
2345. First I menaced merrily with a feigned one,
And rent thee with no rough-sore, with right I proffered it thee
For the compact that we made fast on the first night,
And thou trustily and truly the troth held with me,
All the gains thou gave me, as a good man should.
2350. That other feint I proffered thee was for the morn, man,
When thou kissed my fair wife — the kisses given me.
For both those two I bid thee here but two bare feints
                    without scathe.
            A true man restores truly,
2355.   Then that man dreads no danger.
            Thou failed there at the third,
            And therefore that tap took thee.

XVI

'For it is my weed that thou wearest, that same woven girdle,
Mine own wife gave it thee, I wot well forsooth,
2360. Now know I well thy kisses, and thy traits also,
And the wooing of my wife: I wrought it myself.

I sent her to assay thee, and soothly I think thee
One of the most faultless men that ever went on foot;
As a pearl beside the white peas is of more worth,
2365. So is Gawain, in good faith, beside other gay knights.
But here you lacked a little, sir, and loyalty you wanted;
But that was for no wily workings, nor for wooing neither,
But for ye loved your life; the less I blame you.'
That other sturdy man stood in study a great while,
2370. So aggrieved with anger that he raged within;
All the blood of his breast rushed to his face,
So that he shrank for shame at what the man said.
The very first words that the knight spoke were:
'Cursed be cowardice and covetousness both!
2375. In you is villainy and vice that destroys virtue.'
Then he caught at the knot, and loosens the form,
Flung fiercely the belt at the man himself:
'Lo, there is the false thing, may evil befall it!
For care of thy blow taught me cowardice
2380. To accord me with covetousness, my nature to forsake,
Which is the largesse and loyalty that belongs to knights.
Now I am faulty and false, and afeard have been ever
Of treachery and untruth: may sorrow and care
                    betide both!
2385.   I confess to you, knight, here still,
                 All faulty is my fare;
                 Let me regain your goodwill
                 And then I shall beware.

XVII

Then laughed that other man and lovingly said,
2390. 'I hold it handily whole, the harm that I had.
Thou art confessed so clean, aware of thy offenses,
And have had the penance plain from the point of my blade,
I hold thee purified of that plight, and washed as clean

As if thou had never transgressed since thou was first born;
2395. And I give thee, sir, the girdle that is gold-hemmed;
For it is green as my gown, Sir Gawain, ye may
Think upon this same contest, where you press forward
Among prized princes, and this a pure token
Of the adventure of the green chapel between chivalrous knights.
2400. And ye shall in the New Year come again to my dwelling
And we shall revel the remnant of this rich feast
full well.'
There invited him eagerly the lord
And said, 'With my wife, I ween,
2405. We shall you well accord,
That was your enemy keen.'

XVIII

'Nay, forsooth,' quoth the man, and seized his helm,
Takes it off kindly, and thanks the knight;
'I have sojourned long enough; happiness betide you
2410. And may he grant it you soon who grants all honors!
And commend me to that courteous one, your comely wife,
Both that one and that other, mine honored ladies,
That thus their knight with their scheme have quaintly beguiled.
But it is no wonder that a fool should act madly
2415. And through the wiles of women be won to sorrow,
For so was Adam on earth with one beguiled,
And Solomon with many and sundry, and Samson besides —
Delilah dealt him his fate — and David thereafter
Was blinded by Bathsheba, and suffered much woe.
2420. Now if these men were vexed with their wiles, it were a huge win
To love them well and believe them not, if a man could do that.
For these were the noblest of old, that all the fortune followed
Excellently of all those others, under heaven's kingdom
that mused.

2425.   And they all were beguiled
                 With women that they used.
                 Though I be now beguiled
                 I think I ought to be excused.

XIX

           'But your girdle,' quoth Gawain, 'God repay you for that!
2430. That will I wield with good will, not for the fair gold,
           Nor the belt itself, nor the silk, nor the side pendants,
           For neither wealth nor honor, nor for the fine works,
           But as a sign of my trespass I shall see it oft,
           When I ride in renown, recall with remorse
2435. The fault and the faintness of the crabbed flesh,
           How tender it is to entice traits of filth;
           And thus, when pride shall prick me for prowess of arms,
           The look at this love-lace shall humble my heart.
           But one thing I would you pray, if it displease you not:
2440. Since ye be lord of the land yonder where I spent time
           With you with honor — may the wight repay you it
           That upholds the heaven and on high sits —
           How do ye say your right name, and then no more?'
           'That shall I tell thee truly,' quoth that other then,
2445. 'Bertilak de Hautdesert I am called in this land.
           Through the might of Morgan le Fay, that in my house stays,
           And by cleverness of lore, by crafts well learned,
           The many masteries of Merlin has acquired —
           For she has dealt in love-making full dear at times
2450. With that knowledgeable scholar, that knows all your knights
                  at home.
             Morgan the goddess
             Therefore is her name:
             None wields such high haughtiness
2455.   That she cannot fully tame —

XX

'She sent me in this guise to your goodly hall
For to assay the arrogance, if it were sooth,
That runs of the great renown of the Round Table.
She had me perform this marvel to steal your wits,
2460. For to have grieved Guinevere and cause her to die
With horror of that same man that ghostly spoke
With his head in his hand before the high table.
That is she that is at home, the ancient lady;
She is even thine aunt, Arthur's half-sister,
2465. The duchess of Tintagel's daughter, that dear Uther after
Begat Arthur upon, that now is king.
Therefore I ask thee, knight, to come to thy aunt,
Make merry in my house; my household loves thee,
And I will thee as well, wight, by my faith,
2470. As much as any man under God for thy great troth!'
And he answered him nay, he would not by no means.
They embrace and kiss and commend each other
To the prince of paradise, and part right there
in the cold;
2475. Gawain on his horse well-fed
To the king's castle hastens bold,
And the knight in the emerald-green
Goes whithersoever he would.

XXI

Wild ways in the world Gawain now rides
2480. On Gringolet, that the grace had gotten of his life;
Oft he harbored in house and oft all thereout,
And had many adventures in this vale, and vanquished oft,
That I do not intend at this time in the tale to recount.
The hurt was whole that he had received in his neck,
2485. And the shining belt he bore thereabout
Aslant as a baldric bound by his side,

Locked under his left arm, the lace, with a knot,
To betoken he was taken in the taint of a fault.
And thus he comes to the court, a knight all sound.
2490. Weal wakened there when the great ones wist
That good Gawain was come; a gain they thought it.
The king kisses the knight, and the queen also,
And then many a sure knight that sought him to hail,
And about his journey asked him; and wonderfully he tells,
2495. Confessing all the types of trouble he had had,
The adventure of the chapel, the cheer of the knight,
The love of the lady, lastly the lace.
The nick on the neck he naked them showed
That he received for his disloyalty at the lord's hands
2500.   as reproof.
              He was vexed when he must tell,
              He groaned for grief and wrath;
              The blood rushed to his face,
              When he must show it, for shame.

XXII

2505. 'Lo, lord,' quoth the man, and the lace handled,
'This is the band of this blame I bear in my neck,
This is the injury and loss that I have suffered
For the cowardice and covetousness that I have caught there,
This is the token of untruth that took me in,
2510. And I must needs wear it while I may last.
For a man may hide his harm, but may not undo it,
For where it once is attached it will never sever.'
The king comforts the knight, and all the court also
Laugh loudly thereat, and lovingly agree
2515. That the lords and ladies that belonged to the Table,
Each member of the brotherhood, a baldric should have,
A band aslant about him of a bright green,
And that, for the sake of that man, to wear it in suit.
For that was accorded the renown of the Round Table,

2520. And he that had it was honored evermore after,
       As it is related in the best book of romance.
       Thus in Arthur's day this adventure befell,
       The Brutus books bear witness thereof;
       Since Brutus, the bold warrior, first bent his course hither,
2525. After the siege and the assault was ceased at Troy,
                    indeed,
            Many adventures here before
            Have so befallen ere this,
            Now he that bore the crown of thorns
2530.   May he bring us to his bliss! AMEN.

HONY SOYT QUI MAL PENCE.

Printed in the United States
By Bookmasters